Classica

A Child's Guide t

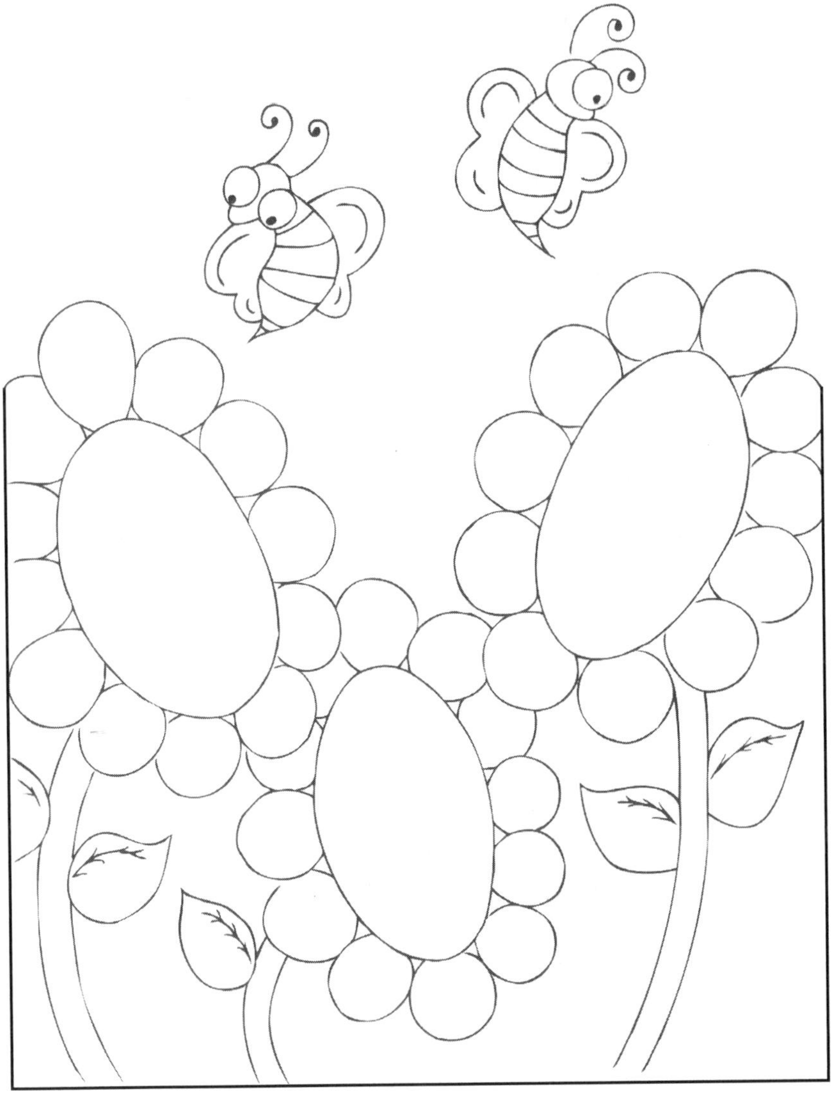

Cheryl Lowe

Classical Phonics

A Child's Guide to Word Mastery

Published by:
MEMORIA PRESS
www.memoriapress.com

ISBN #978-1-61538-011-4

Illustrated by Starr Steinbach and Karah J. Force
Cover Design by Karah J. Force

Contents

Preface, 1913

This little book is intended to be put into the hands of children at the beginning of their first year in school. It may be used in conjunction with any series of readers.

Teachers generally recognize the value of a good foundation in phonics as an important aid in learning to read. Unfortunately many teachers are not sufficiently familiar with the principles underlying phonic analysis and the building of words to feel sure that they can make their phonic drills as economical and as effective as they should be. Pupils, therefore, often fail to get sufficient phonic practice to become proficient in word recognition. Moreover, no matter how helpful the readers may be in suggestions as to teaching phonics, it devolves upon the teacher to prepare a great deal of phonic work. This requires much time and energy, as it must of necessity be presented to the pupils from the blackboard, or from large printed cards and charts. It has seemed to the author that it would be a great advantage to both teacher and pupil to have before the pupil, in a book, a carefully worked out and thoroughly tested series of exercises in phonics, which have been found to make pupils self-reliant in word mastery.

The author has evolved this system of teaching phonics in her own schoolroom and has found that it ensures rapid progress in learning to read. It is presented to her fellow teachers with the hope that it may serve to lighten their burdens and bring to them greater success in the fine art of teaching reading.

*Do not undertake to teach these lessons until you have carefully studied the "Suggestions to Teachers," pages 122-126.

Florence Akin

Preface, 2010

Many years ago I ordered Florence Akin's *Word Mastery*. It was a pint-sized little book with lists of words and some pencil sketches and little else, or so I thought. When it came in the mail I was a little disappointed, looked at it briefly, laid it aside, and forgot about it for several years. One day, after I had learned much more about phonics, I picked it up again and spent some time with it, reading the introduction and teaching instructions, turning the pages slowly, studying the order and manner of its presentation, reading the little comments at the bottom of each page. I began to realize that the simplicity of *Word Mastery* is deceiving. *Word Mastery* is in fact a little gem, a well-organized and methodical presentation of phonics based on years of experience. It is all you really need in order to teach phonics. *Word Mastery* focuses on what is most important, and that only, becoming a very effective guide to learning and understanding phonics. Once you as a teacher learn how to distinguish between the essential and the fluff, you can always add your own bells and whistles without sacrificing the effectiveness of your lesson.

We have made many improvements in the appearance and organization of *Word Mastery*, adding design and graphics to make pages more attractive, substituting our own hand-drawn pictures for the older sketches, some of which would be perplexing to today's children, reducing the number of words per page, and reorganizing word groups to make them easier. The last half of the book had a very loose organization, which has been extensively reorganized to make it more understandable and phonetically accurate in agreement with the pronunciation guide of the *American Heritage Dictionary*. A page of sight words that do not fit into any phonetic word group in English is another addition we have made. In fact we made so many improvements to the original *Word Mastery* that we decided to name our new edition *Classical Phonics*. We believe the wise and sensible order of phonics principles as well as the simplicity of presentation make *Classical Phonics* deserving of its name.

What makes *Classical Phonics* so effective? *Classical Phonics* is a compilation of phonics in one little book and thus gives the teacher and the student the advantage of having both the whole and the parts presented visually in one small concise book. It is made to put into the hands of children, but gives you as a teacher all you need to teach and understand phonics. With *Classical Phonics* you can see the whole scope of phonics and also each part in its relation to the whole, developing real understanding and in-depth knowledge.

A second reason that *Classical Phonics* is so effective is its word family lists. Learning a sound, its phonogram, and a list of words to illustrate that phonic principle is what phonics is all about. Word lists are not all that exciting, but they are a great aid in learning to read, and they produce rapid progress. The word lists are made for the children, and although there are innumerable other props you could use, nothing is more effective than word lists. They are direct and to the point.

At Highlands Latin School in Louisville, Kentucky, we have used *Classical Phonics* as a supplement to our reading program in K-2. I incorporated the first section of *Classical Phonics* into *First Start Reading*, thinking we would not need *Classical Phonics* until the first grade, but I was mistaken. The kindergarten teachers and parents still wanted their *Classical Phonics* books, and I soon discovered why. When each *First Start Reading* workbook was completed and put away, the students still needed their word lists to practice previously learned phonics and compare new words to old ones. The beautiful simplicity of *Classical Phonics* keeps everybody focused. It is a compendium of all of the phonics the child learns in K-2 in a handy little review book. Whatever phonics program you are using, *Classical Phonics* can be your vademecum (go with me) review book for years to come.

Classical Phonics is not a complete language program. It does not provide sentences for reading or printing lessons. However, to add these elements would, I think, decrease its effectiveness.

Classical Phonics is an accurate window into the best of the reading instruction that was common at the turn of the century, before look-say and whole language methods were introduced into American schools.

I hope our updated *Classical Phonics* helps you become a more effective reading teacher and helps your students make more rapid progress in learning to read.

Cheryl Lowe

Part One

Unit 1

Alphabet

Short Vowels

CVC Words

M, n, r, f, s, l represent sounds that may be prolonged, or voiced without a vowel sound. This makes them the easiest of the consonant sounds to blend, and therefore the first to learn. If you have not read both prefaces and the teaching suggestions on page 122-126 please do so before proceeding any further.

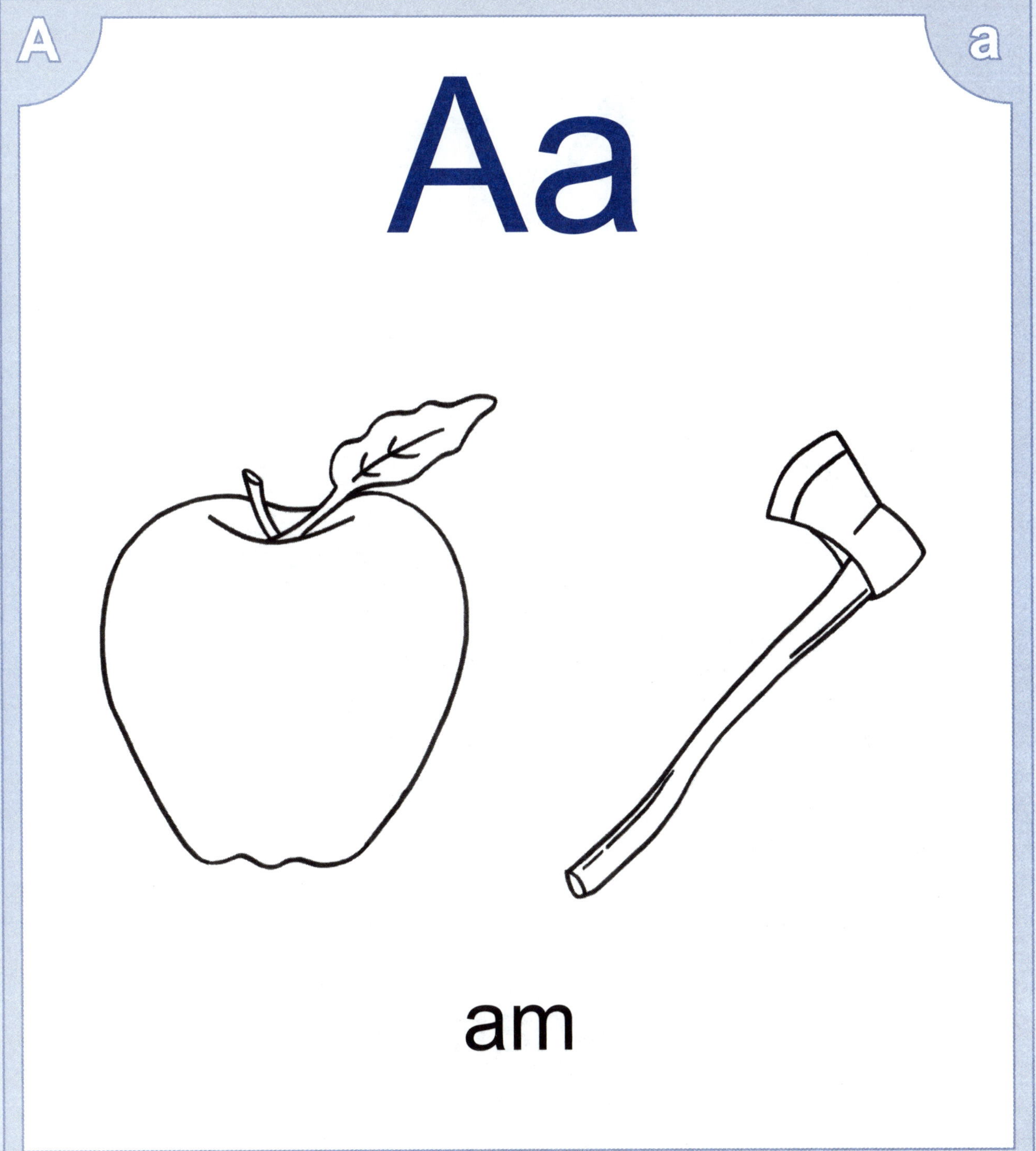

A is the first short vowel studied. Pupils can remember the sound of short **a** by isolating the initial sound of the word **apple**. Pupils can now blend two letters to make the word **am** and use it in a sentence: **I am** (child's name).

N n

Nn

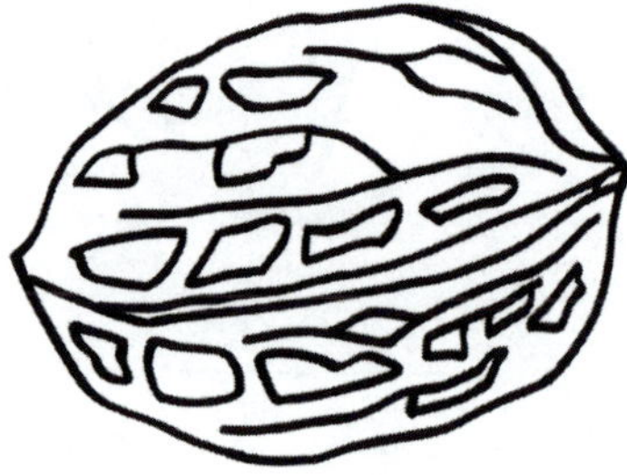

man

Isolate the initial sound of **nest** and **nut**. Pupils can now blend the three letters they have learned to make the word **man**. **M** and **n** have similar sounds. Help students enunciate each sound clearly.

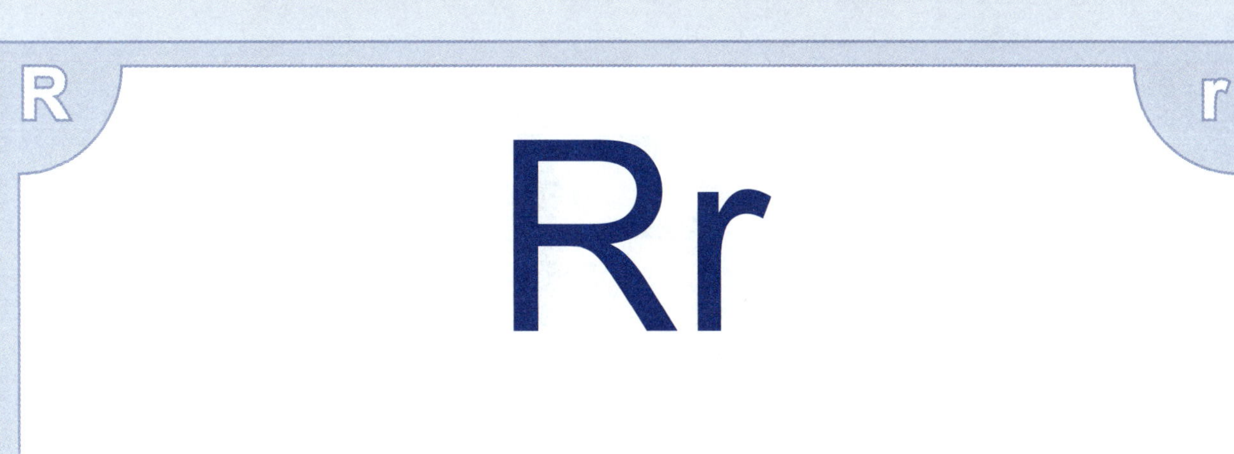

ran ram

Isolate the initial sound of **ram**, **rat**, and **rose**. Pupils now know four letters and can blend two more words, **ran** and **ram**.

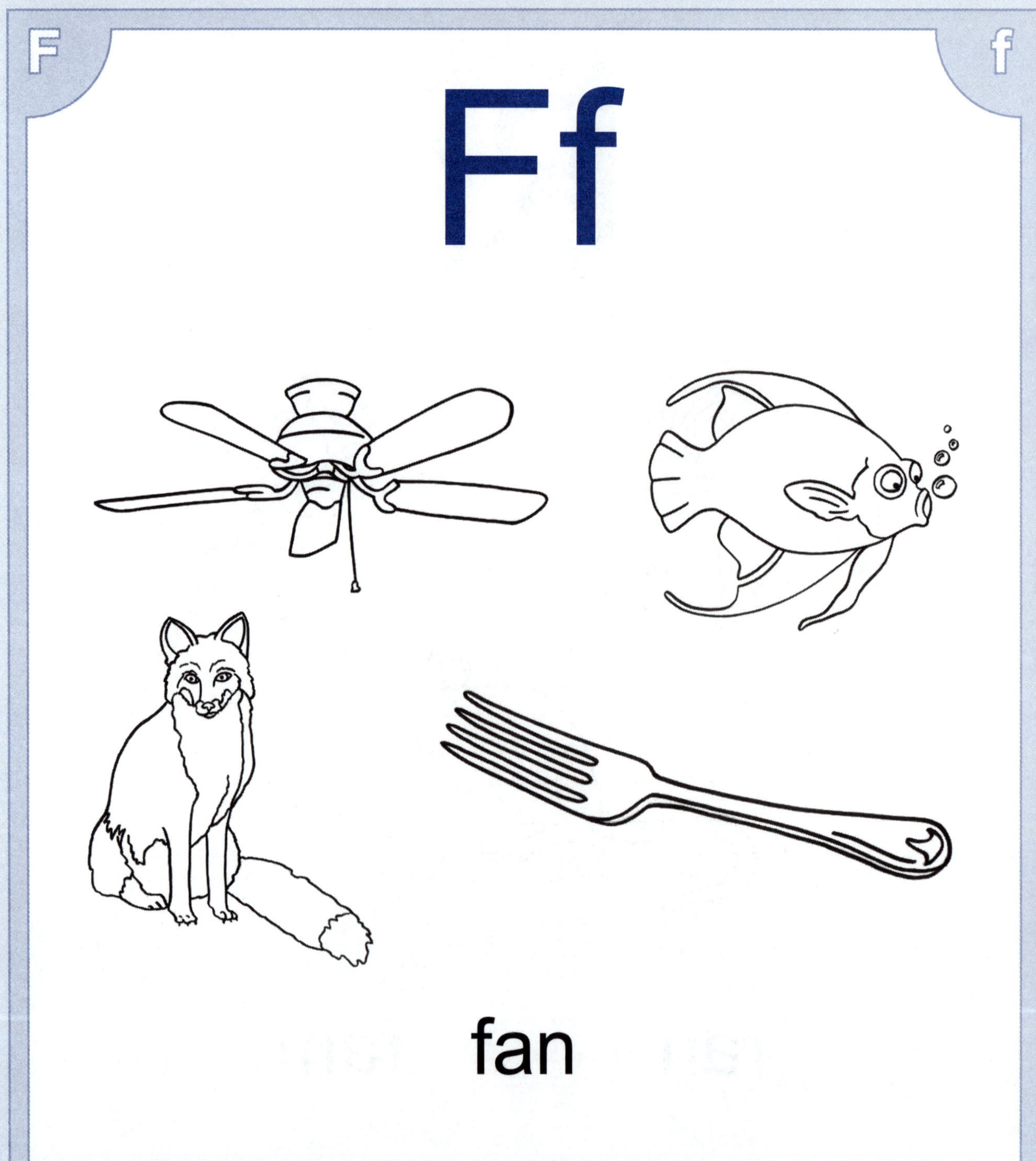

Isolate the initial sound of the words for these pictures. Pupils can now blend the word **fan**.

S s

Ss

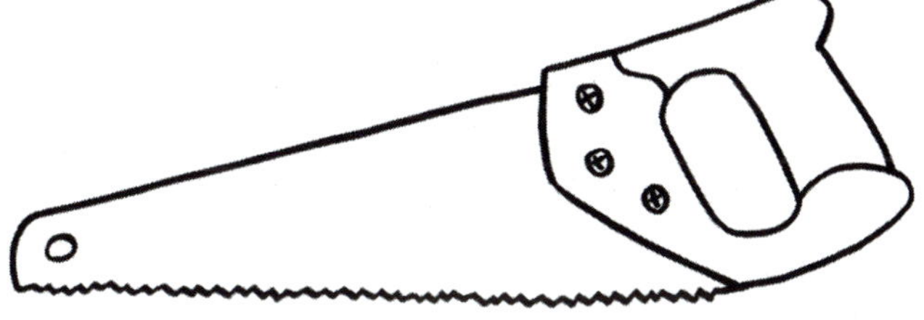

Sam

Isolate the initial sound of the words for these pictures. Pupils can now blend the word **Sam**. Ask pupils why **Sam** begins with a capital.

E e

Ee

men	ran
man	man
fan	men
Sam	fan
ran	Sam

E is the second vowel studied. Pupils can remember the sound of short **e** by isolating the initial sound of the word **egg** or **Ed**. Take each step slowly at first. Lay the foundation well. Practice each column for mastery.

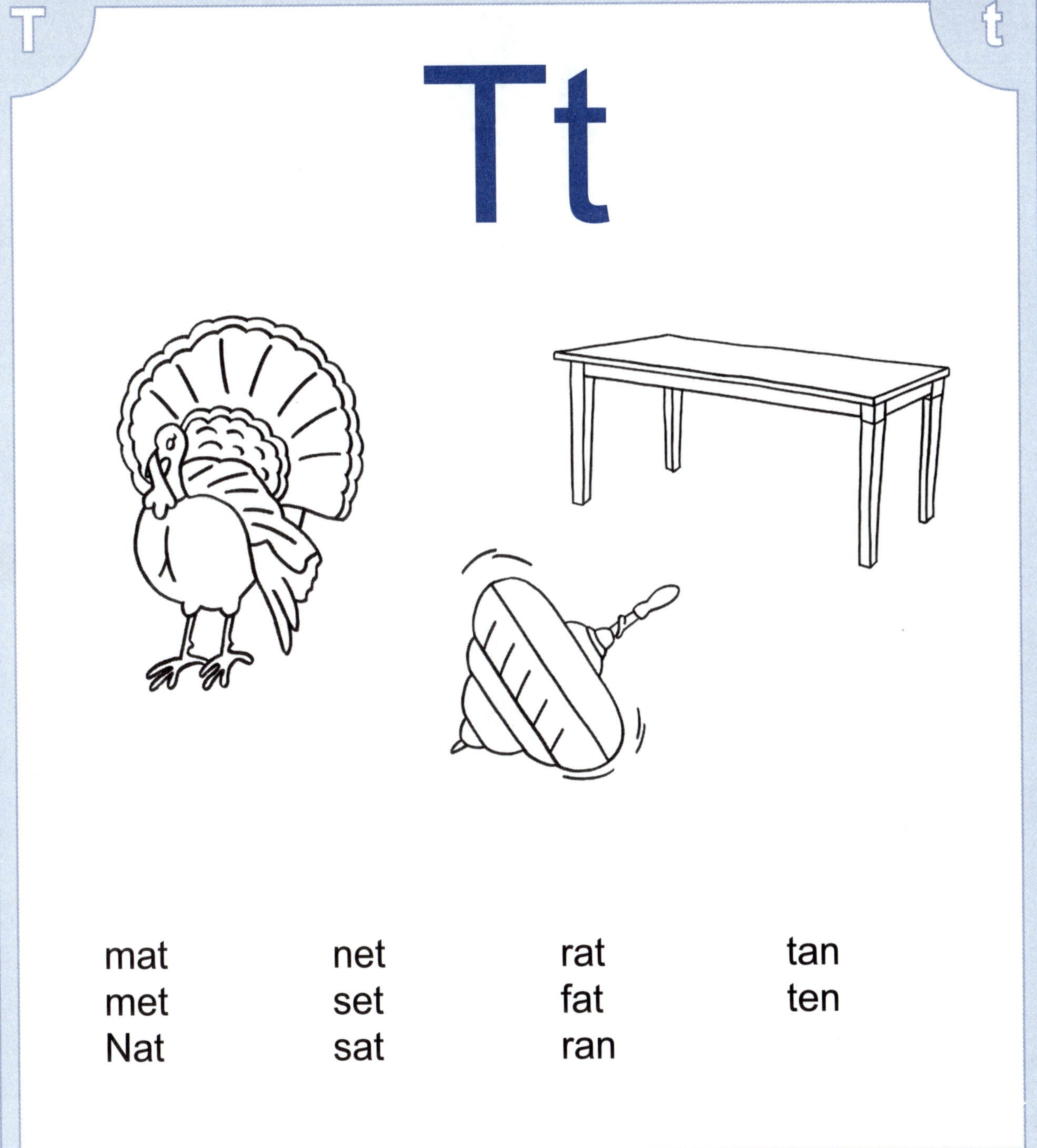

T, used first as a terminal, then as an initial sound. Practice these word lists until pupils demonstrate mastery. Use words in sentences.

Isolate the initial sound of the words for these pictures. The sound of **l** can be a difficult one for children to say and blend.

G, used first as a terminal, then as an initial sound. Only the hard sound of **g** is given in the beginning.

Cc

cat can

Only the hard sound of **c** is given in the beginning.

Kk

keg

The letter **k** and hard **c** have the same sound.

B b

Bb

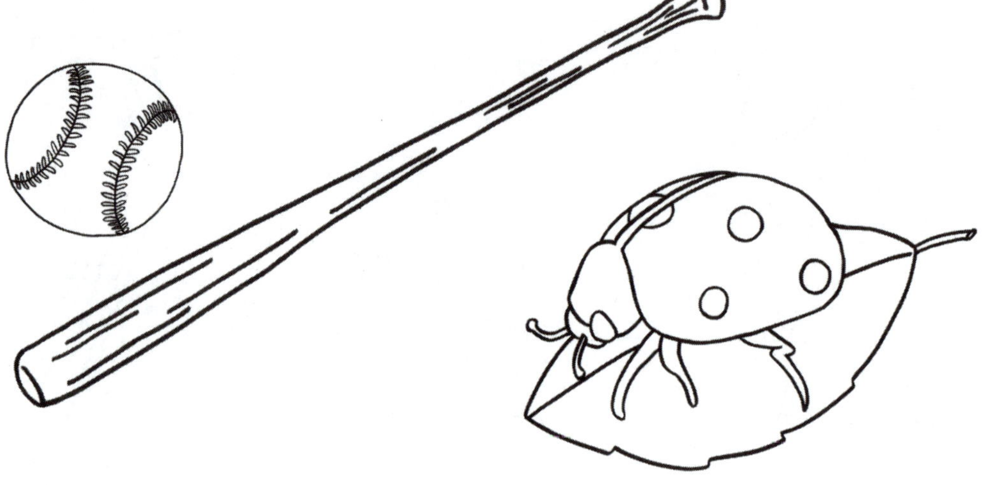

cab bat
Tab bag
Ben beg

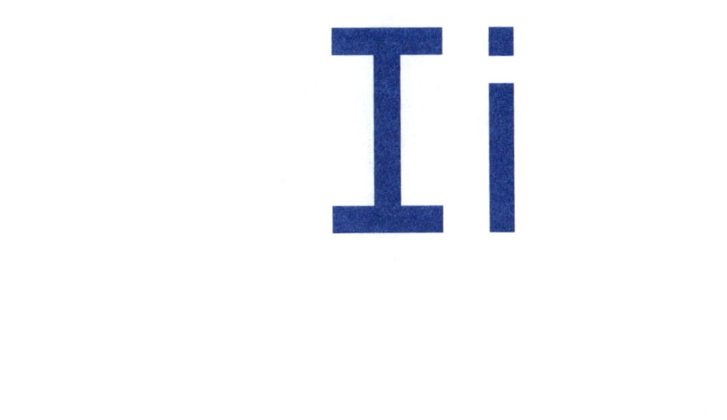

bit
bat
sit
sat
set

fig
tin
ten
tan
fit

fat
rib
bib
big
beg

bag
fin
rim

I is the third vowel studied. Pupils can remember the sound of short **i** by isolating the initial sound of the word **igloo** or **inchworm**. These pages require much patience and care. Go slowly now, and speed will come later.

H h

Hh

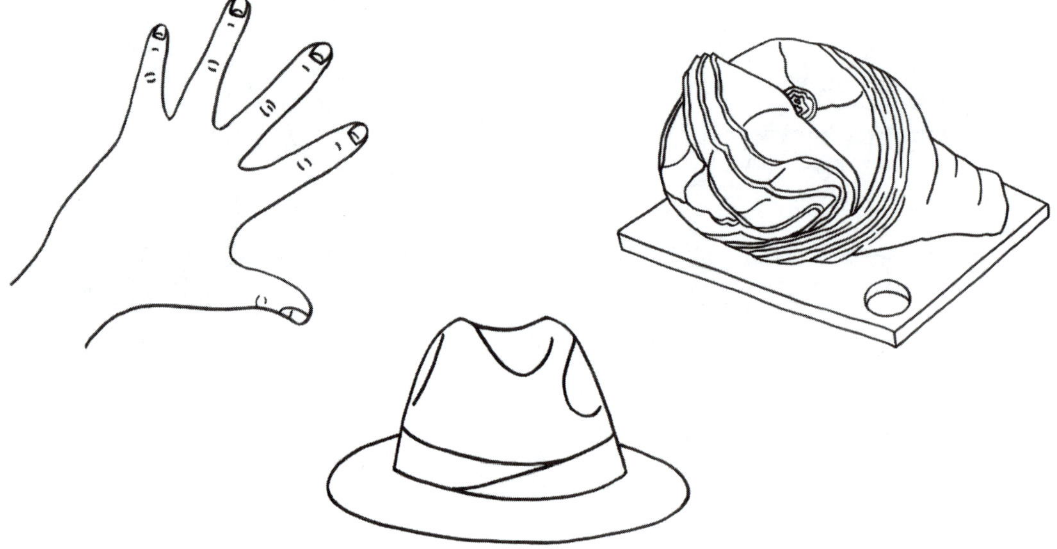

hat	ham
hit	him
hem	hen

D d

Dd

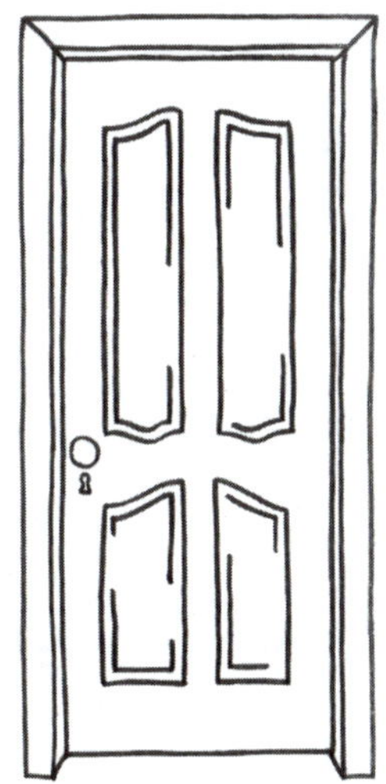

red	fed	bed	din
rid	hid	bad	dig
lad	had	sad	dim
led	mad	did	
lid	mid	den	

The short sounds of **e** and **i** are very close. Practice these word lists carefully. If pupils confuse lowercase **b** and **d**, draw a **bed** poster that pupils can see at all times. Say **b** comes before **d**, and **b** looks like the head board and **d** is the footboard.

P p

Pp

tap	nap	hip	pit
tip	map	pan	pig
rip	lap	pin	peg
rap	lip	pen	
sip	cap	pet	
sap	dip	pat	

Oo

log
fog
fig
cob
cab
rob
rib
nod
sod

pod
pad
rod
rid
red
hop
hip
lap
lip

lop
top
tap
tip
got
pot
pat
pet
pit

hat
hit
hot
let
lot
dot

O is the fourth vowel studied. Pupils can remember the sound of short **o** by isolating the initial sound of the word **ostrich** or **octopus**.

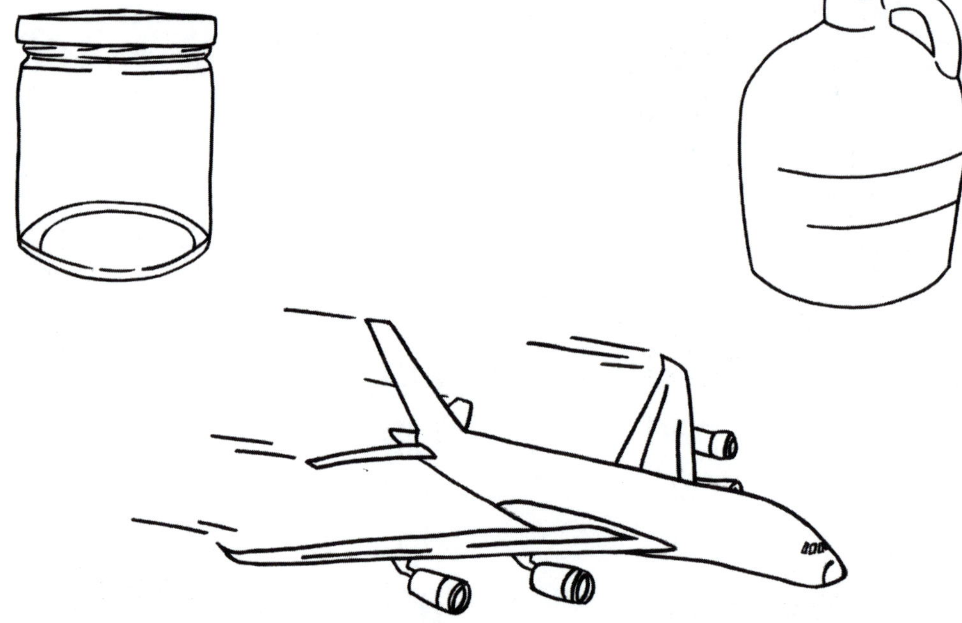

jam jet

W w

Ww

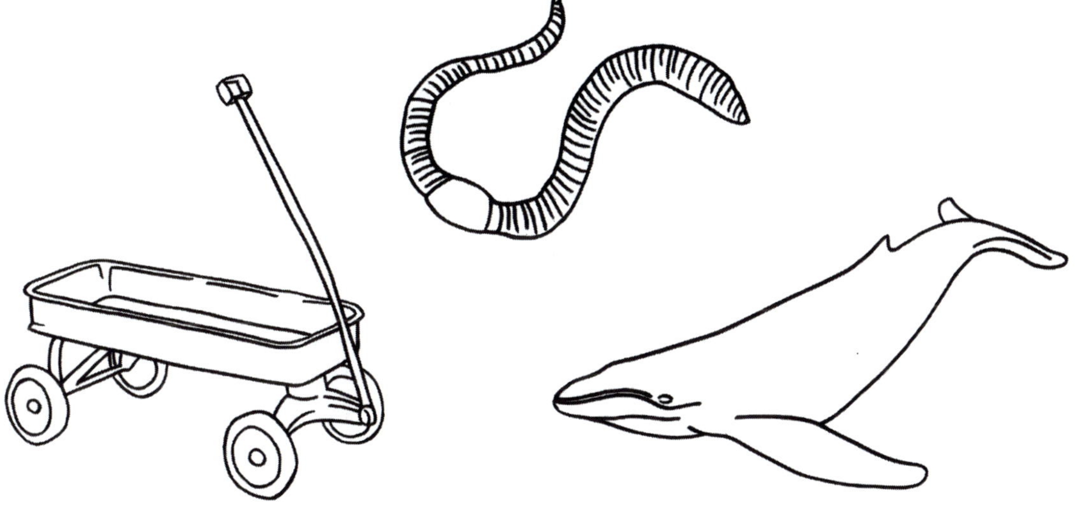

wag	wet
wig	web
wit	win

U u

Uu

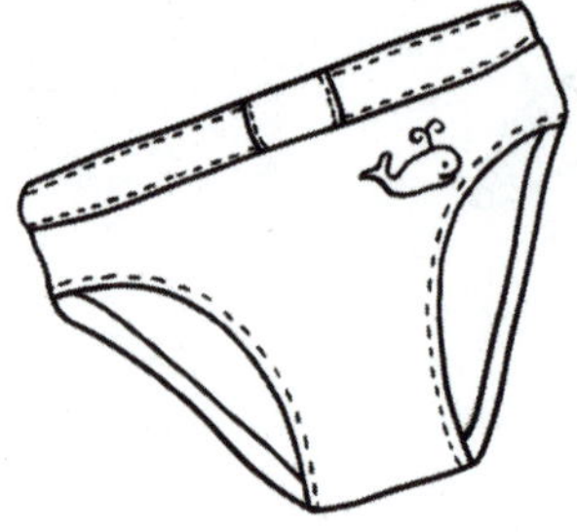

gum	rug	rub	gun
hum	hug	mud	sun
hem	jug	bud	cut
ham	pug	sup	hut
him	peg	cup	hat
bug	pig	pup	hot
beg	tag	run	hit
bag	tug	bun	but
big	tub	Ben	nut
rag	hub	fun	

U is the fifth vowel studied. Pupils can remember the sound of short **u** by isolating the initial sound of the word **umbrella**.

Z z

Zz

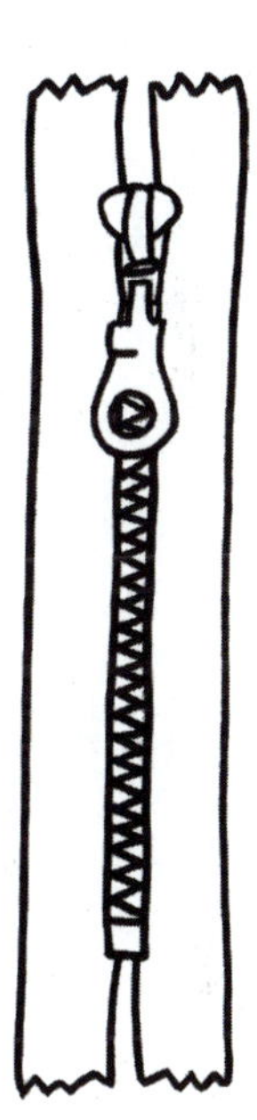

zig zag

X 

x = /ks/

ax
box
fox

fax
fix
six

X is a single letter for the consonant blend **ks**. These words have the sound of **x** as the terminal consonant. There are no words that begin with the sound of **x**.

Q is always followed by **u**, and **qu** represents the consonant blend **kw**.

V V

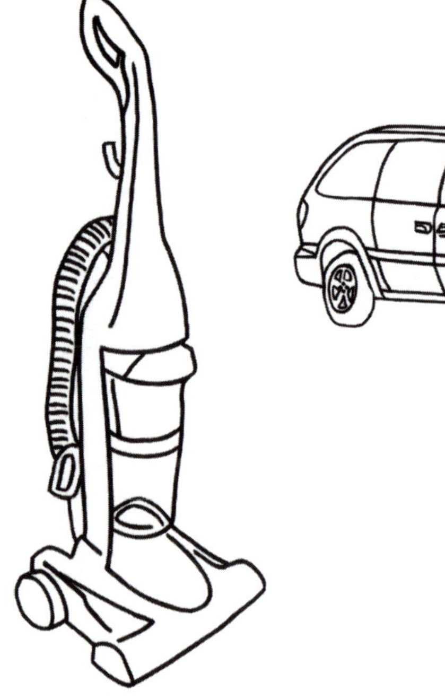

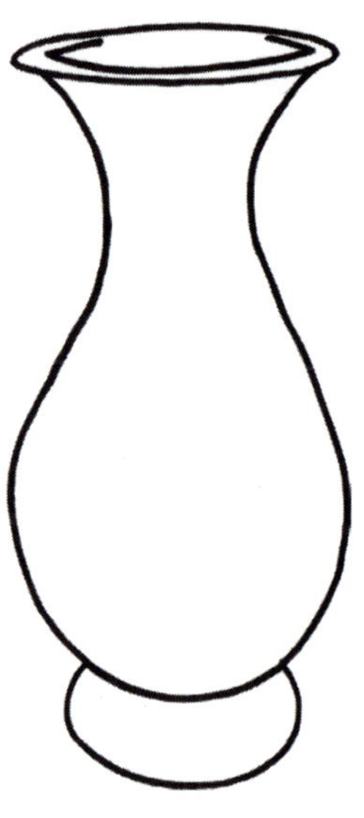

vat van

Only the consonant sound of **y** is given in the beginning.

Review A: CVC words arranged in word families

a	e	i	o
at	n et	it	d ot
c at	p et	b it	h ot
b at	g et	h it	l ot
h at	l et	s it	p ot
s at	w et	w it	c ot
m at	s et	f it	t ot
p at	m et	p it	n ot
r at			g ot
	h en	in	
an	m en	p in	h op
c an	p en	t in	m op
f an	t en	s in	p op
m an	B en	w in	t op
p an	d en	f in	l op
r an			s op

All of the words we have studied are called consonant-short vowel-consonant words, or CVC words. Practice the words on these three pages to mastery. **Phonics Rule #1:** The vowel in a CVC word or syllable is short.

Review A: CVC words arranged in word families

u	a	e	i
ut	c ap	r ed	h id
c ut	l ap	l ed	d id
n ut	m ap	f ed	l id
b ut	n ap	b ed	m id
r ut	g ap	N ed	b id
h ut	s ap		k id
	t ap	h em	r id
s un	r ap		
g un		b eg	d ip
f un	b ad	l eg	h ip
r un	h ad	k eg	l ip
b un	m ad	p eg	r ip
	s ad		t ip
up	p ad	w eb	p ip
c up	l ad		s ip
p up		R ex	
s up		v ex	

It is helpful to read and review phonics rules, but asking students to memorize them is not necessary.

Review A: CVC words arranged in word families

o	u	a	i
p od	b ud	am	h im
r od	m ud	j am	r im
n od		h am	d im
s od	g um	S am	
	h um		b ig
h og		t ag	d ig
f og	b ug	b ag	p ig
l og	r ug	w ag	f ig
	h ug	r ag	w ig
c ob	m ug	s ag	j ig
r ob	j ug		
m ob	p ug	c ab	b ib
s ob	t ug	T ab	r ib
ox	t ub	ax	s ix
b ox	r ub	w ax	m ix
f ox	h ub	t ax	f ix

When pupils have mastered the rhyming word families in Review A, proceed to Review B, where the same words are grouped by the initial letter.

Review B: CVC words grouped by beginning letter

an	c up	g as	if
at	c ut	g et	it
am		g ot	in
ax	d en	g um	
	d ip	g un	j am
b at	d id		j et
b ad	d ig	h at	j ug
b ag	d im	h ad	
b ed	d ot	h am	k eg
b ig	d in	h en	
b it	d ug	h id	l ad
b ox		h im	l ap
b ug	f an	h ip	l et
	f at	h it	l ed
c ab	f ed	h op	l ip
c at	f ig	h og	l id
c an	f in	h ot	l og
c ap	f it	h ug	
c ob	f og	h um	m an
c ot	f ox	h ut	m ad
c ub	f un		m ap

Review B: CVC words grouped by beginning letter

m at
m en
m et
m ix
m ud

n ap
n et
n od
n ot
n ut

on
ox

p an
p at
p eg
p en
p et
p ig

p in
p od
p op
p ug

r ag
r ed
r im
r ip
r ob
r ug
r un

s ad
s ag
s ap
s et
s in
s it
s ix
s ob

s op
s un

t ag
t an
t ap
t ax
t en
t in
t ip
t op
t ub
t ug

up
us

v an
v at
v ex

w ag
w ax
w eb
w et
w ig
w in

y es
y et

z ig
z ag

When pupils have mastered these two reviews, you are ready for the final assessment on the following page. Congratulate your pupils. They have mastered one sound for each consonant and the all-important short vowel sounds.

Assessment: CVC Words

1	2	3	4
can	lid	bed	mix
hub	mat	fig	tub
ham	Ben	rob	box
zag	run	vex	log
pop	let	jug	cab
lip	win	rib	hem

5	6	7	8
rot	Tom	top	red
beg	yes	cup	big
fed	rug	tip	keg
sit	Nan	yet	bat
did	sad	wax	ten
tug	map	kid	led

Assessment. Your pupil should be able to read these words accurately before proceeding to the next section. Re-teach, review, and practice until s/he has mastery of these phonic principles.

Part One

Unit 2

Long Vowel Sounds

Silent **e** Words

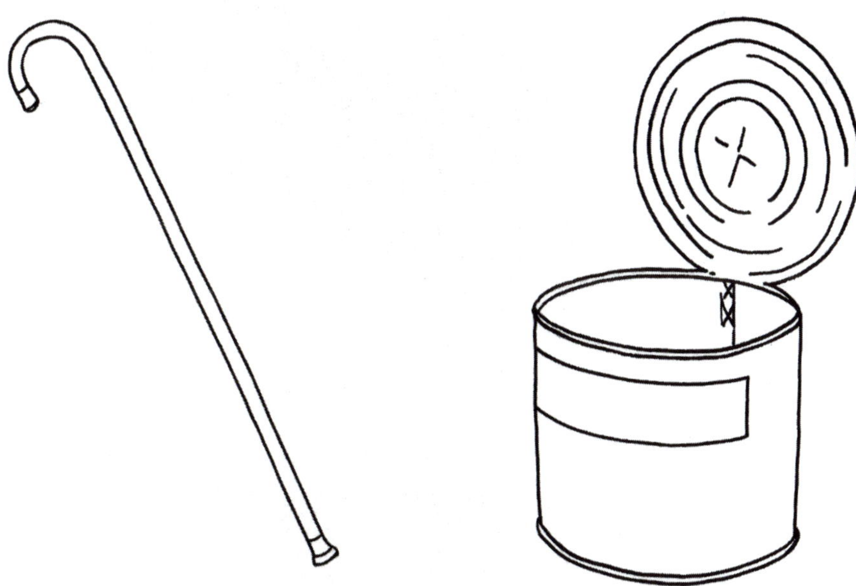

Silent e Words

at	m an	d im	b it
ate	m ane	d ime	b ite
h at	c ap	f in	r id
h ate	c ape	f ine	r ide
m at	t ap	p in	r od
m ate	t ape	p ine	r ode
r at	S am	t in	r ob
r ate	s ame	t ine	r obe
f at	m ad	w in	h op
f ate	m ade	w ine	h ope
c an	f ad	d in	m op
c ane	f ade	d ine	m ope
p an	h id	r ip	l op
p ane	h ide	r ipe	l ope

The long vowel sounds are the same as the letter names. **Phonics Rule #2:** Silent **e** at the end of a one-syllable word makes the vowel before it say its name. Each pair of words illustrates the power of **magic e**.

Silent e Words

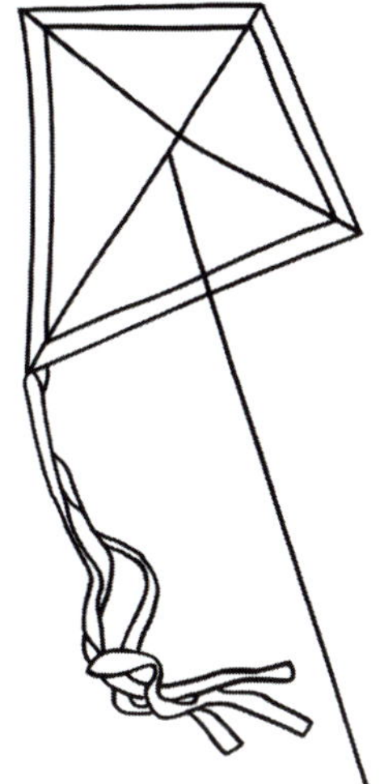

n ot	us
n ote	use
c ut	c ub
c ute	c ube

---

a

r ake	l ate	c ame	p ave
w ade	c ase	g ale	t ame
s afe	v ase	p ale	J ane
b ake	K ate	s ale	l ane
c ake	c ave	n ame	w ave
l ake	d ate	t ale	b ase
t ake	g ate	g ame	s ave
m ake	g ave	l ame	g aze

Practice these **silent e** words to mastery.

Silent e Words

o	u	i	i
p oke	m ule	s ide	w ipe
j oke	m ute	w ide	k ite
y oke	c ute	t ide	f ire
p ole	f use	l ife	m ire
h ole	use	w ife	w ire
m ole	c ure	f ile	t ire
b one		l ime	h ire
c one	t ube	t ime	
t one	r ule	m ine	
r ope	r ude	l ine	
h ome	t une	v ine	
d ome	d uke	n ine	
	J une	f ive	
		h ive	
		d ive	
		l ive	

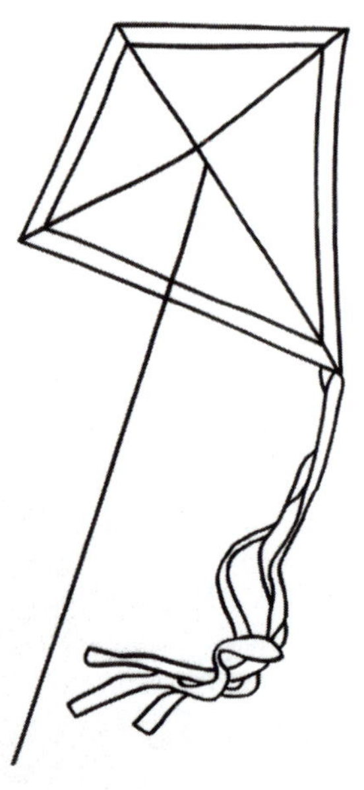

Long **u** has the sound of its name (**yoo**) in some words: *mule* (myool), *mute*, *cute*, *fuse*, *cure*.
Long **u** also has the sound of long **oo** (*boot*) in other words: *tube* (toob), *rule*, *rude*, *tune*, *duke*, *June*.

Silent <u>e</u> Words Review

late
mine
gave
bite
pole
cane
wire
dime
hope
pure
wore
line

bone
rake
wove
time
hive
mane
rate
cone
yoke
pane
pile
more

ride
tire
pipe
lake
pine
ripe
tone
life
home
cape
date
robe

cure
dive
fade
gate
rode
vane
hire
ate
cute
cake
rope
vase

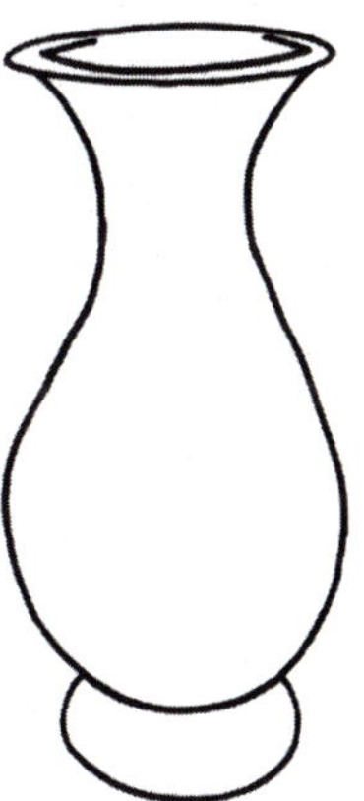

Review of long vowel sounds without separating the phonograms. Practice for the assessment on the following page.

Assessment: Silent e Words

1

kite
make
same
safe
sale
pale

2

save
fate
hide
wake
Kate
side
lame

3

mate
cave
take
wide
gaze
wife
lane

4

mule
pave
name
bale
here
came
use

5

vote
sake
make
lone
wade
case
dose

6

note
Jane
cure
wave
size
use
nine

7

hole
tame
wine
pure
tape
wipe
bale

8

fuse
tide
cone
mute
vine

Assessment. Your pupil should be able to read these words accurately before proceeding to the next section. Re-teach, review, and practice until s/he has mastery of these phonic principles.

Part One

Unit 3

Plurals

Possessives

Final Consonant Teams & Blends

Plurals and s = /z/

plurals			s =/z/
cat	pipe	rakes	is
cats	pipes	rats	his
		makes	as
cap	bite	wipes	has
caps	bites	jokes	
		bakes	nose
sit	rope	tips	rose
sits	ropes	dates	pose
		cups	
dip	yoke	wakes	rise
dips	yokes	kites	wise
		wets	
top		hopes	use
tops		taps	fuse
		fits	muse
nut		pets	
nuts		maps	
gate			
gates			

Most words form their plurals by adding **s**. **S** often has the sound of **z**.

Possessives

Ned's cap

Kate's rose

Tom's cane

Jane's cake

Dan's fox

Dave's home

Nat's box

Bob's top

Ben's cup

Sam's bat

Ted's dime

mule's rope

cat's bed

hen's leg

man's gun

pig's pen

The singular possessive is formed by adding 's.

CVCC Words: final **ck** and double **l, s, f, z**

ck	ll	ff	ss
b ack	b ell	b uff	k iss
l ack	f ell	c uff	m iss
p ack	s ell	m uff	h iss
s ack	t ell	p uff	m oss
t ack	w ell	h uff	l oss
d eck	y ell	off	t oss
n eck	N ell		l ess
p ick	ill	**zz**	B ess
l ick	b ill	b uzz	m ess
k ick	f ill	f uzz	p ass
t ick	h ill	j azz	f uss
s ick	k ill	f izz	
l ock	m ill		
r ock	t ill		
b uck	w ill		
d uck	J ill		
	d oll		
	d ull		

Look back on pages 36-38. Notice that there are no words that end in **k, l, s, f,** or **z**. **Phonics Rule #3:** In one syllable words, the final **l, s, f,** and **z** are doubled. **Phonics Rule #4:** The final **k** in one-syllable words is spelled **ck**. All of these words have short vowel sounds. **Quiz** and **whiz** are exceptions.

CVCC Words: final consonant blends - **nd, nt, st, mp**

nd	nt	st	mp
and	b ent	f ast	b ump
h and	r ent	l ast	d ump
l and	s ent	p ast	j ump
s and	t ent	b est	l ump
b and	w ent	n est	p ump
end	h unt	t est	c amp
b end	h int	w est	d amp
m end	l int	r est	l amp
s end	m int	v est	r omp
w ind	t int	l ist	l imp
		f ist	
		m ist	
		c ost	
		d ust	
		m ust	
		r ust	
		j ust	

Phonics Rule #5: The vowel in **CVCC** words is usually short. Pupils should practice blending the two consonants so closely that they form one continuous sound.

CVCC Words: final consonant blends - **ft, pt, xt, lt, lf, lk, lp**

ft

g ift
l ift
r ift
s ift
l oft
s oft

pt

k ept
w ept

xt

n ext
t ext

lt

f elt
m elt
b elt
w ilt

lf

elf
s elf
g olf

lk

b ulk
s ilk
m ilk
e lk
h ulk

lp

h elp
y elp

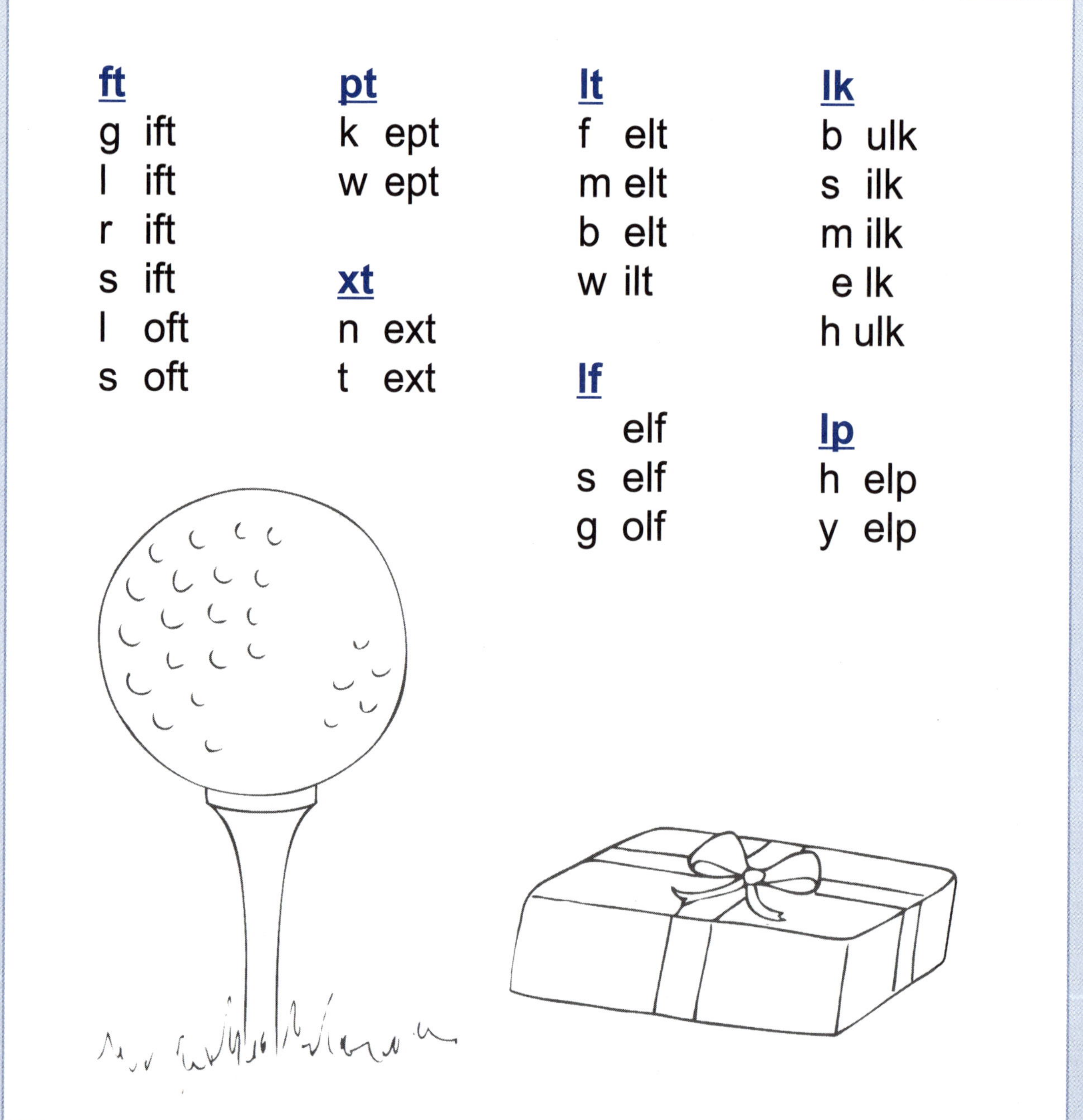

Pay particular attention to the four **l** blends. **L** has two sounds, **luh** at the beginning of a word and **uhl** after a vowel. The **l** sound after a vowel can be particularly difficult for children. Practice these words orally with your pupil until s/he masters them.

Assessment: CVCC Words, Plurals, and Possessives

west	elk	Bill	fuzz
moss	left	well	camp
next	huff	duck	must
mock	jump	limp	kept
send	went	elf	help
belt	off	hand	milk
hint	back	soft	sent
Ned's cap	sits	cakes	Sam's bat
rose	use	as	is
has	wise	his	nose

Assessment. Your pupil should be able to read these words accurately before proceeding to the next section. Re-teach, review, and practice until s/he has mastery of these phonic principles.

Part One

Unit 4

Consonant Teams

ch, **sh**, **th**, **wh**

&

Initial Consonant Blends

s, **r**, **l** blends

Consonant Teams: ch and sh

ch

ch in
ch ap
ch ip
ch at
ch op

ch eck
ch ick
ch ill

ch ase
ch ime
ch oke

s uch
m uch
r ich

nch

b ench
l unch
b unch
p unch

tch

p atch
l atch
c atch
h atch
m atch

itch
w itch
p itch
h itch

n otch
b otch
D utch

sh

sh ip
sh od
sh ed
sh ot
sh op
sh un
sh ut

sh ock
sh ell
sh elf

sh one
sh ape
sh ame
sh ave
sh ine
sh ore

ash
l ash
m ash
s ash
c ash
d ash

d ish
w ish
f ish

h ush
r ush

There are 4 major consonant teams: **ch, sh, th, wh**. These teams are phonograms for consonant sounds not covered by any of our 26 letters. A consonant team is not a blend, like the ones students have just learned. Try blending these consonant teams to illustrate this to students. Note: **nch** is a blend of the letter **n** before **ch**, and in **tch** the **t** is silent before **ch**.

Consonant Teams: th and wh

th		wh
th in	ten th	wh ip
th ick	ma th	wh im
th ump	pa th	wh en
	ba th	wh et
th e	mo th	wh iz
th at	wi th	
th en	wid th	wh ich
th is		wh ack
th an		wh iff
th us		wh ile
th em		wh ite
		wh ine
th ese		wh ale
th ose		
th ine		

The vowels on these two pages can be long or short. Help your pupils apply the **silent e rule** to determine the correct pronunciation of each word. There are two sounds for **th**—the voiced (*the*) and the unvoiced (*thin*). It is often necessary for a pupil to sound the word both ways in order to discover the correct pronunciation.

Assessment: Consonant Teams - **ch, sh, th,** and **wh**

shake	math	catch	shine
while	white	these	witch
chin	much	then	fish
which	when	this	check
shift	with	than	lunch
pitch	shelf	tenth	whim

Assessment. Your pupil should be able to read these words accurately before proceeding to the next section. Re-teach, review, and practice until s/he has mastery of these phonic principles.

Initial Consonant Blends: s-blends - sc, sk, sm, sn, sp, st

sc

- sc at
- sc um
- sc ant
- sc amp

- sc ore
- sc ale

sk

- sk ip
- sk im
- sk in

- sk iff
- sk ill
- sk ull

- sk ate
- sk etch

sm

- sm ell
- sm elt
- sm ash
- sm ack
- sm ith
- sm ile
- sm oke

sn

- sn ug
- sn ag
- sn ap
- sn iff
- sn uff
- sn atch

- sn ake
- sn ipe
- sn ore

sp

- sp ot
- sp un
- sp in
- sp an
- sp ill
- sp ell

- sp eck
- sp end
- sp ade

- sp ike
- sp ire
- sp ite
- sp ine
- sp oke

st

- st op
- st ub
- st ab
- st ep
- st em
- st iff
- st uff
- st ill
- st ilt
- st ack
- st ick
- st uck
- st amp
- st omp
- st ump
- st and
- st ove
- st one
- st ate
- st itch

Initial consonant blends are grouped in three categories: **s-blends, r-blends, l-blends**. Pupils should practice blending the two consonants so closely that they form one continuous sound. The vowels in these words can be long or short. Help your pupil apply the **silent e rule** to determine the correct pronunciation of each word.

Initial Consonant Blends: r-blends - **br, cr, dr, fr, gr, pr, tr**

br

br ag
br im
br ick
br ush
br isk
br ake
br ave
br ide
br oke

cr

cr ab
cr op
cr ib
cr ack
cr aft
cr isp
cr ane
cr ept
cr ush
cr ate

dr

dr ag
dr ess
dr ift
dr ill
dr ive
dr op
dr ove
dr ug
dr um
dr ip
dr ape
dr one

fr

fr og
Fr ed
fr om
fr ost
fr oze
fr esh
fr ame

gr

gr ip
gr it
gr in
gr ill
gr ass
Gr eg
gr and
gr asp
gr ade
gr ape
gr ove

pr

pr od
pr int
pr ess
pr ick
pr ide
pr ize

tr

tr ap
tr im
tr ip
tr od
tr ot

tr ack
tr ick
tr uck
tr amp
tr ash
tr ade

In the **r-blends**, **r** is the second lettter. Pupils should practice blending the two consonants so closely that they form one continuous sound. The vowels in these words can be long or short. Help your pupil apply the **silent e rule** to determine the correct pronunciation of each word.

Initial Consonant Blends: l-blends - bl, cl, gl, fl, pl, sl

bl

bl ed
bl ot

bl ess
bl ock
bl ack
bl uff

bl ade
bl ame
bl aze

bl unt
bl ush
bl and
bl end

cl

cl ap
cl ip
cl od
cl ub
cl am
cl an

cl uck
cl ick
cl ock
cl one
cl ose
cl utch

gl

gl ad
gl ass
gl ade
gl ide
gl obe
gl aze

fl

fl ag
fl at
fl ax
fl it
fl op
fl ap

fl ock
fl ake
fl ame
fl esh
fl ash

pl

pl an
pl ot
pl um
pl ate
pl ant
pl ush

sl

sl at
sl ab
sl ip
sl am
sl id
sl it
sl im
sl ed

sl ack
sl ide
sl ate
sl ave
sl ope
sl ash

In the **l-blends**, **l** is the second lettter. The vowels in these words can be long or short. Help your pupil apply the **silent e rule** to determine the correct pronunciation of each word. Pupils may find these more difficult than the **s** and **r** blends.

Assessment: Initial Consonant Blends

black	clam	globe	flag
bled	close	glad	flash
plate	slim	scamp	skin
plant	slide	score	sketch
smell	sniff	spell	stop
smile	snore	spend	stomp
brag	crack	dress	from
bride	craft	drop	froze
grin	print	truck	step
grass	pride	tramp	drive

Assessment. Your pupil should be able to read these words accurately before proceeding to the next section. Re-teach, review, and practice until s/he has mastery of these phonic principles.

Part One

Unit 5

More Consonant Blends: **sw**, **tw**

Three-Letter Blends

Consonant Teams: **qu**, **nk**, **ng**

More Consonant Blends: sw, tw, qu, squ

sw	tw	qu	squ
sw am	tw ig	qu ack	squ id
sw an	tw ill	qu ill	squ ish
sw ell	tw ine	qu ilt	squ int
sw ept	tw ist	qu it	
sw im	tw it	qu ite	
sw um	tw ins	qu iz	
sw ine	tw itch	qu ick	
sw ift			
sw ore			
sw itch			

The letter **q** is always followed by the letter **u**. **Qu** is a phonogram for the blend **/kw/**.

More Consonant Blends: three-letter blends

scr
scr ap
scr ape
scr atch
scr ub

shr
shr ub
shr ill
shr imp
shr ed
shr ug

spl
spl ash
spl it
spl int

spr
spr ig
spr ite

str
str ap
str ip
str ipe
str ive
str ide
str ike
str oke
str etch

thr
thr ob
thr ill
thr ift
thr ash
thr ush
thr ust
thr ive
thr one

Three-letter blends take practice. Take your time and go slowly.

Consonant Team: ng

ang	ing	ong	ung
bang	sing	long	hung
hang	ring	song	rung
rang	king	gong	sung
gang		bong	lung
	string		
clang	sling	prong	stung
sprang	wring	strong	swung
	thing	tongs	slung
			sprung
			strung

Try to sound out **bang** phonetically (**ban g**) and you will see that the **ng** represents a special sound, **/ng/**. Do not try to isolate or analyze this difficult sound for your pupil. Just pronounce and practice the endings **ang**, **ing**, **ong**, and **ung** correctly, and s/he will be able to read these words.

Consonant Team: nk

ank	ink	onk	unk
bank	ink	honk	sunk
blank	link	bonk	dunk
clank	sink		bunk
plank	mink		chunk
rank	pink		flunk
crank	drink		junk
Frank	think		
thanks	blink		
drank	chink		
sank	shrink		
tank			

Try to sound out **bank** phonetically (**ban k**) and you will see that the **nk** has a special sound. The letter **n** in these words has **/ng/**, and thus **nk** becomes **/ngk/**. Do not try to isolate or analyze this sound for your pupil. Just pronounce and practice the endings **ank**, **ink**, **onk**, and **unk** correctly, and s/he will be able to read these words.

Assessment: More Consonant Blends and Endings

swam	twig	quack	shrub
swine	twitch	quick	shrimp
splash	scrap	sprig	strap
split	scrape	sprite	stretch
thrill	hang	sing	long
throne	clang	thing	strong
lung	blank	pink	honk
sprung	thanks	shrink	junk

Assessment. Your pupil should be able to read these words accurately before proceeding to the next section. Re-teach, review, and practice until s/he has mastery of these phonic principles.

Part One

Unit 6

Three Sounds of **y**

Long Vowel Teams

ai and **ay = /ā/**

ea and **ee = /ē/**

oa = /ō/

Long **i** and **o** in CVCC Words

Three Sounds of y

y (consonant)	long i	long e	
yes	by	candy	foggy
yet	my	dusty	bunny
yell	cry	copy	merry
yelp	dry	Henry	chilly
Yale	fly	sixty	Betty
yoke	fry	ninety	Polly
yam	pry	twenty	sorry
yak	sly	fifty	penny
	spy	baby	
	thy	frisky	
	try	slimy	
	why	busy	
	shy	juicy	
	sky	sunny	
	bye	puppy	
	eye	kitty	
	buy	cherry	
	cyclone	fluffy	
		funny	
		jolly	

Y can be a consonant or a vowel. Students have learned the consonant sound, and here they are introduced to the two vowel sounds of **y**, long **i** and long **e**.

Long Vowel Teams: ai and ay = /ā/

ai

aid
m aid
l aid
p aid
br aid
afr aid

ail
fail
bail
rail
hail
jail
mail
nail
sail
pail
snail

aim
claim

gain
rain
drain
brain
grain
train
main
strain
sprain
pain
lain
plain
slain
chain
stain

faint
paint
quaint

raise
praise

waist

bait
gait
wait
strait

ay

b ay
d ay
r ay
tr ay
g ay

gray
hay
lay
clay
may
pay
play
pray
say
stay
stray
way

There are about 25 vowel teams in English. Helping students master these vowel teams will greatly enhance their reading and spelling skills. For the vowel teams taught in this unit, the first vowel is long and the second is silent. These words obey the well-known rule "When two vowels go walking, the first does the talking." This rule is helpful for now, but warn students that we will see many exceptions later.

Long Vowel Teams: ea = /ē/

sea
tea
flea

each
peach
beach
reach
teach

read
bead
lead

leaf

leak
beak
peak
speak
sneak

streak
squeak

heal
meal
seal
steal
squeal

beam
seam
team
steam
stream
dream

bean
lean
mean
clean

heap
leap
cheap
reap

ear
fear
near
tear
dear
year
clear
shear

ease
easy
tease
please

east
beast

feast
yeast

eat
beat
heat
meat
neat
seat
cheat
treat
wheat

leave
weave

The vowel teams taught in this unit represent one speech sound. They are not blends like the consonant blends previously studied. Teach students that a **macron** over a vowel, as shown for **ā**, **ē,** and **ō**, indicates a long vowel.

Long Vowel Teams: ee = /ē/

ee			
s ee	seek	deep	breeze
f ee	week	keep	freeze
b ee	cheek	sheep	sneeze
w ee	meek	steep	squeeze
fl ee		creep	
free	eel	peep	beech
glee	feel		leech
three	heel	deer	speech
	peel	cheer	screech
r eed	steel		
deed		beet	
feed	seem	feet	
need		meet	**final e**
seed	seen	sheet	he
weed	keen	fleet	she
bleed	green	greet	we
	sheen	sweet	be
reef	queen	street	me
beef	screen		the

Long Vowel Teams: oa = /ō/

l oad
r oad
t oad

loaf

oak
cloak
croak
soak

coal
goal

foam
roam

loan
moan

oat
coat
float
goat
boat
throat

roast
toast
coast
boast

roach
coach
poach

Vowels i and o: may be long when followed by two consonants

long i	long o		
mild	old	roll	colt
wild	told	toll	jolt
child	cold	stroll	bolt
	gold		
bind	hold	post	both
blind	mold	most	
find	sold		
hind	scold		
kind			
mind			
wind			
grind			

Phonics Rule #6: The vowels **i** and **o** may be long when followed by two or more consonants. This is an exception to **Phonics Rule #5**. Distinguish between the two words *wind* (long **i**) and *wind* (short **i**).

Assessment: Long Vowel Teams and Three Sounds of Y

yes	candy	puppy	by
yet	penny	sixty	my
cry	why	maid	rain
bye	sky	snail	strain
day	sea	clean	please
pray	each	year	eat
need	sweet	road	goat
cheek	screech	croak	roast
mild	kind	old	stroll
blind	wind	hold	most

Assessment. Your pupil should be able to read these words accurately before proceeding to the next section. Re-teach, review, and practice until s/he has mastery of these phonic principles.

Part Two

Unit 7

Soft **c** and **g**

More Long Vowel Teams

Soft c: c and **sc** are soft before **e, i**, and **y**

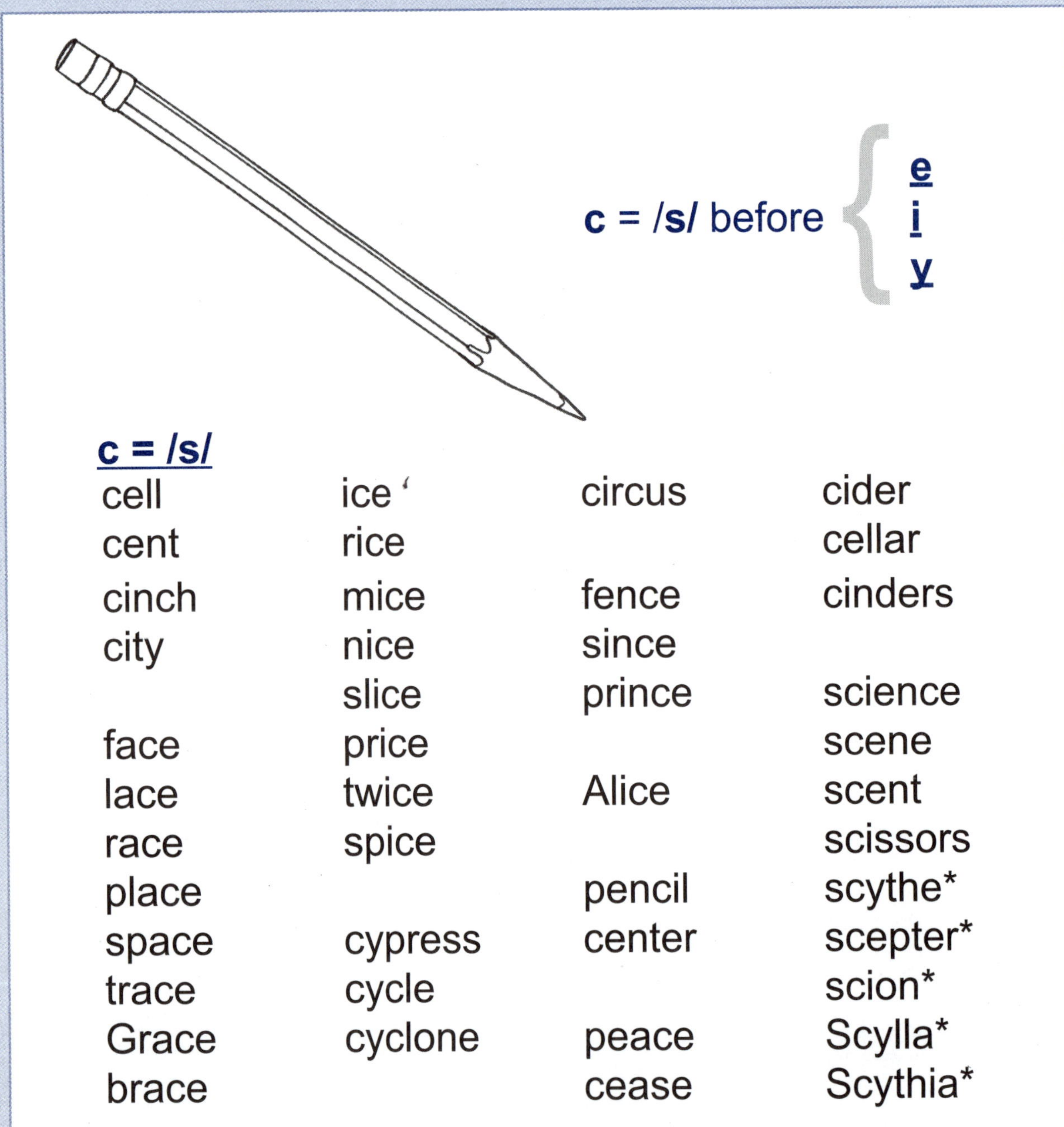

c = /s/

cell
cent
cinch
city

face
lace
race
place
space
trace
Grace
brace

ice
rice
mice
nice
slice
price
twice
spice

cypress
cycle
cyclone

circus

fence
since
prince

Alice

pencil
center

peace
cease

cider
cellar
cinders

science
scene
scent
scissors
scythe*
scepter*
scion*
Scylla*
Scythia*

Phonics Rule #7: c and **g** are usually soft before **e**, **i**, or **y**. Soft **c** = /**s**/ and soft **g** = /**j**/. Students have already learned the hard sound of **c** = /**k**/ and **g** = /**g**/. *Soccer*, *cello*, and *sceptic* are exceptions.

* indicates honors words for older students.

Soft g: **g** is usually soft before **e**, **i**, and **y**

g = /j/ before { e, i, y }

g = /j/

gem
gel
ginger
giraffe
gym
gypsy

giant
gentle
Roger
engine
dingy

ge = /j/

range
change
strange
hinge
gouge
plunge
fringe
forge

age
sage
rage
stage
cage
page
huge

dge = /j/

Madge
badge
edge
ledge
hedge
wedge
fudge
pledge
dredge
ridge
bridge
dodge
lodge
budge
nudge
judge

Common exceptions are: *get*, *girl*, *Gilbert*, *gild*, *gill*.

More vowel teams for /ā/: ei, eigh, ey, ea

ei	eigh	ey	ea
reins	eight	hey	break
reindeer	eighteen	prey	great
veil	eighty	they	steak
vein	weight	grey	
reign	weigh	whey	daybreak
skein	freight		
feign	sleigh		
heir	neigh		
their	neighbor		
beige			

Review the other ways to write /ā/: silent **e** words, page 45; **ai** and **ay**, page 73. The vowel teams presented on this page are exceptions to the "two vowels go walking" rule given on page 73.

More vowel teams for /ē/: ie, ei, ey

ie	ei	ey
chief	weird	donkey
thief	either	chimney
thieves	seize	alley
brief	neither	valley
field	leisure	turkey
priest		honey
	receive	monkey
wield	conceive	volley
yield	deceive	journey
shield	perceive	
grief	ceiling	
grieve		
grieves		
shriek		
piece		
niece		
fierce		

Review the other ways to write /ē/: **ea** and **ee** and final **e**, pages 74, 75; **y**, page 72.
The vowel team **ie** = /ē/ is another exception to the "two vowels go walking" rule.

More vowel teams for / ī /: ie, igh

<u>ie</u>	<u>igh</u>
die	sigh
lie	high
fie	sight
pie	fight
tie	might
	light
	night
	right
	tight
	bright

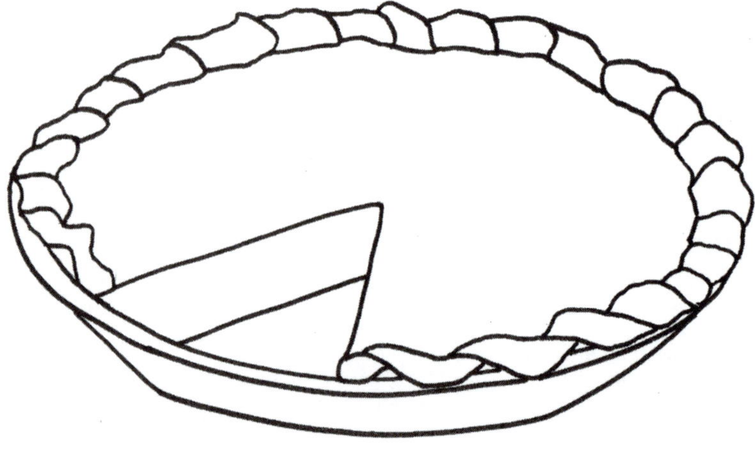

Review the other ways to write /ī/: silent **e** words, page 46; **y**, page 72; exceptions, page 77. Although many of the **vowel teams** in this section include consonants (**ay, ey, ow, aw, oy, igh, ew,** etc.), we will still use the term **vowel team** because they all have at least one vowel and they all represent long vowel sounds.

More vowel teams for /ō/: oe, ow

oe	ow		
toe	owe	mow	mellow
woe	own	mown	yellow
doe		grow	hollow
hoe	bow	grown	
foe	low	throw	window
	tow	thrown	elbow
	row	blow	
	slow	blown	widow
	glow	show	shadow
	crow	shown	
	snow		
	stow	growth	
	flow		
	bowl		

Review the other ways to write /ō/: silent **e** words, page 46; **oa**, page 76; exceptions, page 77.

Assessment: Soft **c** and **g**; More Long Vowel Teams

city cent	ice price	face place	range change
gem gel	fence since	ceiling pencil	piece spice
hey they	break daybreak	reindeer veil	eight neighbor
chief piece	either ceiling	chimney valley	die pie
high night	toe hoe	low slow	yellow shadow

Assessment. Your pupil should be able to read these words accurately before proceeding to the next section. Re-teach, review, and practice until s/he has mastery of these phonic principles.

Part Two

Unit 8

Vowel Teams

for five special vowel sounds

/oi/ /ou/ /o͞o/ /o͝o/ /ô/

Vowel teams for /oi/: oy, oi

oy	oi
toy	oil
boy	toil
soy	soil
coy	boil
Roy	spoil
enjoy	coin
	join
joyful	joint
	point
oyster	
	moist
	noise
	noisy
	choice

All of the previous vowel teams have represented long vowels The vowel teams on these two pages represent two of the five special vowel sounds. /**oi**/ and /**ou**/ are two vowels blended together to make one continuous sound in one syllable. In these *blends* both vowels are heard rather than one being silent.

Vowel teams for /ou/: ou, ow

ou

out
pout
spout
sprout
stout
trout
shout

our
sour
scour
flour

loud
cloud
proud

round
found
mound

pound
bound
ground
sound
wound

count
mount

couch
crouch
pouch
slouch

mouth
south

house
mouse
blouse

ounce
bounce

ow

cow
how
now
bow
brow
plow

owl
howl
fowl
scowl

down
town
clown
frown
crown
brown

crowd

drowsy

The linguistic term for **/oi/** and **/ou/** is **diphthong**. For your pupil, continue to use the term **vowel team**.

Vowel teams for /o͞o/: oo, o

oo

too
boo

boot
toot
root
hoot
shoot

cool
pool
tool
stool
spool

roof
proof

groove

room
boom
bloom
broom
gloom
gloomy

soon
moon
noon
spoon
teaspoon

loop
hoop
coop
droop
stoop
troop
scoop

tooth
smooth
soothe

goose
loose
choose

food

o

do
to
move
prove
shoe

tomb

This sound is actually not new since it is one of the sounds of long **u**. See page 46.

Vowel teams for /o͞o/: ue, ew, ou, ui, u

ue	ew	ui	u
Sue	new	fruit	truth
due	dew	bruise	Ruth
hue	chew	cruise	prune
cue	flew	juice	ruby
blue	stew	juicy	rude
true	drew	suit	rule
clue	grew		ruin
glue	crew		
	strew		
ou	threw		
you	screw		
soup			
croup	few		
group	mew		
youth	pew		
wound			

The vowel teams **ew** and **ou** are exceptions to the "two vowels go walking" rule. Look at the last column. When **u** follows **r** it often has the long **u** sound, **truth**, **Ruth**, etc. **R** is a bossy consonant.

Vowel teams for /ŏŏ/: oo, oul, o, u

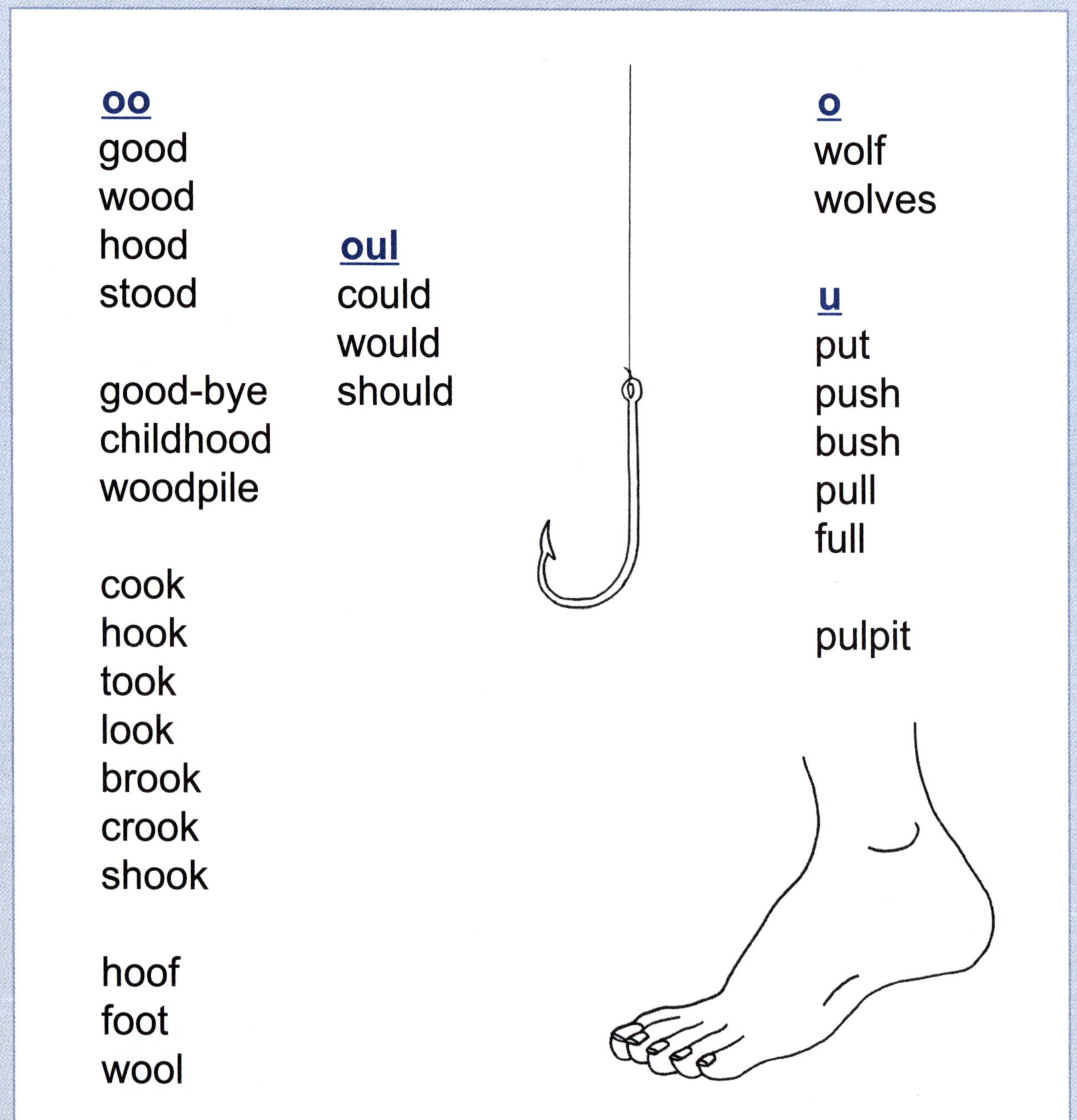

oo

good
wood
hood
stood

good-bye
childhood
woodpile

cook
hook
took
look
brook
crook
shook

hoof
foot
wool

oul

could
would
should

o

wolf
wolves

u

put
push
bush
pull
full

pulpit

This is the fourth new vowel sound. There is no way to predict whether **oo** is long or short. If pupils learn the long sound on the previous page, which is the sound of long **u**, it will bring them close enough that they will be able to get the word. Students can remember *boot* and *foot* for the long and short sounds of **oo**.

Vowel teams for /ô/: all, a, lk, aw

all	al	alk	aw
all	salt	walk	jaw
ball	walnut	talk	law
call	false	chalk	claw
fall		stalk	paw
hall	almost	sidewalk	saw
tall	already		draw
wall	always		straw
stall	altogether		thaw
small			awl
baseball			scrawl
			squaw
all right			shawl
			hawk
			dawn
			lawn
			yawn
			pawn
			awful
			strawberry

The fifth special vowel sound is represented by seven letter teams on this and the next page.

Vowel teams for /ô/: au, aught, ought

au	aught	ought
fault	caught	ought
cause	taught	bought
pause	daughter	brought
gauze		fought
saucer		sought
haul		thought
author		nought
Paul		

Assessment: /oi/, /ou/, /o͞o/, /o͝o/, /ô/

boy	coin	our	down
oyster	choice	cloud	scowl
room	move	wood	blue
tooth	do	look	true
flew	you	fruit	could
few	truth	juice	should
saw	wall	caught	talk
lawn	small	taught	chalk
Paul	thought	false	push
fault	bought		
			wolves

Assessment. Your pupil should be able to read these words accurately before proceeding to the next section. Re-teach, review, and practice until s/he has mastery of these phonic principles.

Part Two

Unit 9

r-Controlled Vowels

/är/ /âr/ /ûr/ /ôr/

&

More Short Vowel Sounds

r-controlled vowels /är/: ar, ä

ar			**ä**
car	arm	large	father
far	farm	charge	aunt
jar	harm		aunt
tar	charm		jaunt
bar			launch
mar	barn		laundry
	darn		grandpa
star	yarn		grandma
starve			
sharp	art		
scar	tart		
card	cart		
hard	dart		
yard	start		
	party		
bark	chart		
dark			
mark	arch		
park	march		
spark	starch		

Words with the broad **a** sound (*father*, etc.) are included here because their sound is similar to the **a** in **ar** words. **R** is one of the *bossy consonants* that pulls the vowels along and controls their sound. *Aunt* is pronounced two ways.

r-controlled vowels /âr/: ar, air, ear, eir, ere

ar
care
dare
fare
hare
bare
rare
ware
glare
spare
flare
snare
stare
share
scare

scarecrow

scarce
square

air
air
hair
fair
pair
stair
chair

stairway

ear
bear
tear
pear
wear

eir
their

ere
ere
there
where

r-controlled vowels /ûr/: ir, ur, or, ear, er

ir

bird
fir
firm
girl
chirp
skirt
shirt
whirl
first
third
thirty
thirst
birth
birthday
squirm
squirrel
circle

ur

bur
fur
blur
slur
sturdy
urge
purse
nurse
churn
burn
turn
hurt
curve
burst
church
purple
turtle
further
nursery

or

word
work
world
worm
worse
worth

ear

earn
learn
earth
heard
pearl
search

er

her
verb
herd
jerk
clerk
term
germ
fern
stern
perch
pert
nerve

r-controlled vowels /ôr/: or, oor, our, oar, ore, war

or

or
nor
for
forth
north
lord
horn
scorn
thorn
form
storm
sort
short
fort
port
sport
snort
cord

force

fork
stork
cork
York
New York
pork
morn
morning
born
corn
torch
scorch
horse

oor

door
floor
poor

our

four
pour
your
fourth
court
course

oar

boar
roar
soar
board
coarse

ore

more
sore
core
shore
chore
fore
tore
swore
store
wore

war

war
warm
swarm
warts

wharf

More Short Vowel Sounds

ea = /ĕ/

head
dead
read
lead

dread
bread
spread
thread

deaf

breast
health
wealth
meant

ready
healthy

ea=/ĕ/

heavy
sweat
breath

meadow
feather
leather
weather

a = /ŏ/

what
want
wad
was
wasp
wash
watch
water

swan
swamp

squash

o = /ŭ/

son
ton
won
none
done
some
come

flood
blood

ou = /ŭ/

touch
young
tough
rough

Pupils have learned that **ea** = /ē/, but here are two more sounds, though neither is as common as the long **e** sound.

Assessment: r-Controlled Vowels; More Short Vowel Sounds

car
park

scare
glare

there
their

world
word

stork
horse

war
warm

was
want
what

charm
party

fair
chair

bird
birth

pearl
search

door
floor

head
read

large
father

bear
wear

fur
purse

verb
germ

your
court

health
ready

son
done

storm
sport

store
more

heavy
breath

flood
rough

Assessment. Your pupil should be able to read these words accurately before proceeding to the next section. Re-teach, review, and practice until s/he has mastery of these phonic principles.

Part Two

Unit 10

Silent Letters

Suffixes

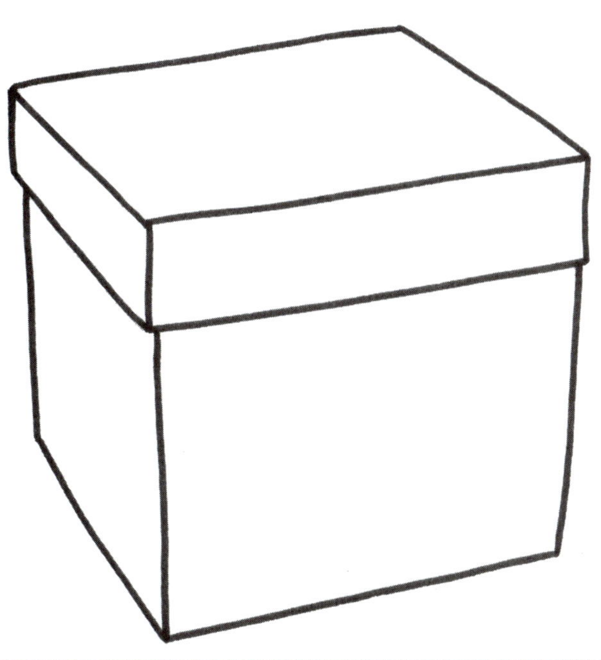

Silent Letters

kn = /n/
knee
knob
knot
kneel
knit
knife
know
knight
knack
knock
knead
knowledge

wr = /r/
wrap
wren
wrench
wring
wrist
wrong
write
wrote
wreath
wreck

mb = /m/
lamb
limb
comb
climb
dumb
crumb
numb
plumbing
thumb
bomb

gn = /n/
sign
gnat
gnash

gu = /g/
guess
guy
guide
guest
guilt

Silent Letters

bu = /b/
build
builder
built
buy

bt = /t/
doubt
debt

silent h
honor
honest
heir
hour
herb
ghost
John
why

silent w
answer
whole
sword
who
whose
whom

silent t
often
listen
hasten
fasten
moisten

Suffix -ed

ed = /ed/	ed = /d/	ed = /t/
petted	sailed	reached
landed	played	puffed
faded	kneeled	baked
tested	plowed	clapped
needed	loaned	ticked
twisted	growled	brushed
wicked	peeled	choked
tinted	frowned	wrecked
	climbed	liked
	pinned	wrapped
	prayed	leaped
	begged	dressed
		packed
		guessed
		dropped
		checked
		dashed
		shipped

The suffix **-ed** has three different sounds depending on the final consonant of the word to which it is added. Since pupils are sounding out words they already know, they should be able to pronounce these words with little difficulty.

Adding the suffix -ing (double or drop)

Double final consonant		Drop silent e	
bat	batting	make	making
mop	mopping	grade	grading
trip	tripping	skate	skating
quiz	quizzing	wave	waving
drop	dropping	hide	hiding
quit	quitting	ride	riding
get	getting	smile	smiling
flip	flipping	shine	shining
grab	grabbing	drive	driving
hop	hopping	hope	hoping
clip	clipping	close	closing
shop	shopping	take	taking
sag	sagging	please	pleasing
		leave	leaving
Never double final w, x, or y		praise	praising
snow	snowing	taste	tasting
box	boxing	paste	pasting
play	playing	dine	dining
		share	sharing
		bite	biting

Adding suffixes to English words is tricky. **Spelling Rule #1:** When adding a suffix that begins with a vowel, double the final consonant of a CVC word, but never double final **w**, **x**, **y**. **Spelling Rule #2:** When adding a suffix that begins with a vowel, drop silent **e**.

Some More Plurals

Change y to i and add -es

candy	candies
carry	carries
story	stories
lady	ladies
penny	pennies
puppy	puppies
berry	berries
copy	copies

Add -es to words ending in s, x, z, ch, sh

church	churches
box	boxes
brush	brushes
dress	dresses
fox	foxes

Unless y follows a vowel

donkey	donkeys
alley	alleys
valley	valleys
boy	boys
play	plays

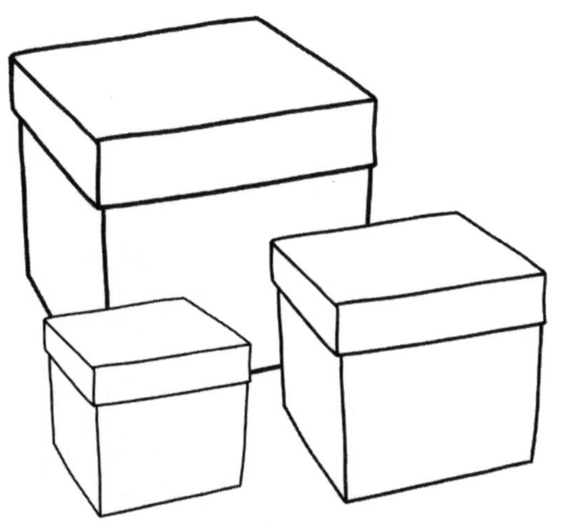

Suffixes -ful, -ly, -less, -ness

ful	ly	less	ness
faithful	safely	useless	kindness
helpful	fully	homeless	illness
careful	sadly	fearless	sadness
playful	gladly	lifeless	goodness
awful	slowly	hopeless	sickness
useful	likely	helpless	madness
thankful	quickly	speechless	
cheerful	lonely		
spiteful	mostly		
truthful	truly		
hateful	bravely		
hopeful	nearly		
restful	neatly		
	gently		
	softly		
	playfully		
	happily		

Spelling Rule #3: Do not change the spelling of a base word when adding a suffix that begins with a consonant. (There are a few exeptions to this rule.) **Spelling Rule #4:** The suffix **ful** has one **l**.

Suffixes with /ər/: er, ar, or

er	ar	or
ever	polar	color
paper	solar	favor
super	dollar	labor
river	beggar	razor
upper	cedar	flavor
singer	grammar	doctor
sister	calendar	actor
winter	pillar	tractor
rocker	liar	error
dinner	burglar	tailor
mother	regular	sailor
brother	hangar	neighbor
flower	collar	
painter		
summer		
cracker		
teacher		

The upside-down **e** is used for a vowel in an unstressed syllable. It has the general sound of short **u**, but varies according to the vowel it represents. The upside-down **e** is called the **schwa** symbol.

Words ending with /ən/: en, in, on, ten

en	in	on	ten
golden	basin	button	glisten
open	raisin	cotton	often
chosen		season	soften
broken		reason	listen
frozen		lesson	hasten
seven		poison	
given		prison	
widen			
kitten			
sweeten			
maiden			
sudden			

Words ending with /əl/: le, el

le

apple
cattle
saddle
cuddle
puddle
kettle
bottle
pebble
riddle
needle
beetle
little
middle
battle
wiggle

able
single
eagle
table
bugle
stable
maple
cradle
tumble
candle
thimble
tangle
twinkle
crumble
handle
people
buckle
pickle
wrinkle
noble

el

travel
angel
chapel
camel
kernel
novel
panel
jewel
nickel
bushel
shovel
label

channel
vessel
flannel
tunnel
barrel
quarrel
squirrel

pretzel
weasel

The two English suffixes **-el** and **-le** have the same sound, **-le** being more common.

Unusual Spellings

ch = /k/

ache
echo
Christ mas
Christ
school
scheme
an chor
stom ach
or chid
choir
cho rus

ch = /sh/

Chi ca go
Char lotte
Mich i gan
Cheryl
chef
par a chute
ma chine
Chev ro let

gh = /f/

laugh
rough
tough
enough
laughter

Unusual Spellings

ph = /f/
phone
or phan
Phil
phon ics
pho to
graph
neph ew
al pha bet
el e phant
Jo seph

ough = /ō/
though
dough
although
thorough
doughnut

i = /y/
onion
union
million
Daniel
warrior
Italian
Spaniard
familiar
companion

Some Common Prefixes

in	**un**	**dis**	**ex**
inside	unable	dismiss	excel
invent	unlike	dislike	except
invite	unwise	disclose	explode
increase	unjust	discolor	explain
incline	untie	discard	express
inquire	unknown	disgrace	expect
	until	discount	excite
	unload	dismay	

Words Accented on Last Syllable

arise
alike
ago
awoke
alone
asleep
afraid
around
away
about
aloud
along
among

before
became
begin
began
begun
behind
belong
behave
below
between
besides
beyond

deceive
decide
delay
delight
declare
depend
desire

obey
object
observe
occur
omit

Assessment: Silent Letters and Suffixes

knob
wrist
thumb
gnat
guess

build
doubt
hour
answer
who
listen

wicked
played
dropped

quitting
boxing
smiling
praising

copies
valleys

brushes
foxes

truthful
neatly

useless
kindness

ever
summer

polar
liar
omit
color
error
neighbor

open
chosen

raisin
season

often
listen

puddle
little

able
candle
people

travel
squirrel

stomach
school

Michigan
laugh
enough

phone
though
onion
familiar
inside

unwise
dislike
except

ago
before
below

decide
behave
obey

Sight Words

I	love	he	to
a	some	she	do
you	come	we	who
of	move	be	two
are	gone	me	too
was	one	the	
were	once	been	no
her	have	eye	so
there	give		go
their	get	does	
here	girl	what	sew
	said		
	says		
	again		
	against		
buy		friend	busy
water	shoe	sure	sugar
though	although	soldier	especially
people	laugh	clothes	special
	length	strength	

Some words on this list are included because they are so common, not because they are unphonetic. Many of the words have pronunciations that contradict rules pupils have learned (*come*, *have*, *said*, etc.) However, except for *eye* and *of*, all of these words have some phonetic elements that pupils can sound out.

Suggestions to Teachers

Do not put this book into the hands of your pupils until you have carefully studied these suggestions.

The following plan approximates the progress of the average primary class. Do not attempt to follow it exactly. Keep in mind the fact that the ability of pupils differs greatly and that whether a class falls behind the suggested plan of work or advances more rapidly, the one important thing is to teach each step thoroughly.

The teaching of phonics includes:

I. Ear training
II. Tongue training
III. Eye training
IV. Word building

Ear Training

Ear training may begin on the first day the child enters school. Say to the pupils:

"We shall play a little game. You may do what I tell you, but do not speak a word."

Then say to one, "*Bring me a* ***b-o-x***."

Speak each **bold** word very slowly (phonetically), emphasizing each sound.

"Show me something ***r e d****. Tap on your* ***d-e-s-k****. Touch something made of* ***t i n****.*
Cl-a-p *your h-ands.* ***R-u-n*** *to the* ***d-oo-r****.* ***H-o-p*** *to the* ***w-i-n-d-ow*** *..."* etc.

Sufficient interest will soon be aroused to permit the teacher to leave off the play and say words phonetically, one after another, asking pupils to tell what each word is. In a few days they will be able to recognize almost any word that may be sounded. Occasionally tell a little story, saying a word phonetically here and there, and allowing pupils to pronounce the word. This form of training may be profitably continued throughout the first half-year.

Tongue Training

Tongue training should begin after ear training. Sound a word and have a pupil tell what sound he hears first, then what sound he hears last. Be very careful that he gives the sound correctly. There is a natural inclination to voice a breath, or voiceless sound, such as **h**. Holding an object before a pupil, have him say the name slowly (phonetically), such as **h-a-t, c-a p, v-a-s-e, p-e-n, b-oo-k, f-a-n,** etc. A picture may be placed before the class, and a pupil may be asked to say phonetically the name of each thing he sees in the picture. After a few days' practice, offer a sound (it may be a simple phonogram, such as **l**, or a compound phonogram, such as **sl**); have the pupils see how many different words they can think of beginning with that sound. This training should be continued for several months. Ear training and tongue training should be practiced continually.

Eye Training

Eye training begins with this book, teaching the pupil to associate the sound with the symbol. Ask the pupil to name the pictures on page 10; he says, **man, moon, mop**. Ask him what sound he hears first (the ear and the tongue training have prepared the way for prompt recognition), and he will reply, **m**. Now tell him that the letters at the top of the page are pictures of the first sound and that hereafter they will help him to tell words. The pupil next learns the sound of **a** in the same way. Then he learns the sound of **n**. Now he says the sounds of the three letters m-a-n, and thereby discovers the word **man**. At first the pupil will say these sounds so far apart that he cannot hear a word, but keep encouraging him to say them more rapidly, as **m---a---n, m--a--n, m-a-n**, until he does hear the word and tells it. Proceed in like manner with the lessons that follow. The order in which the phonograms are presented is based upon the ease with which they are blended.

Eye training begins with this book, teaching the pupil to associate the sound with the symbol.

Word Training

This phonic course contains over 2000 different words. When presented, each of these words contains one new phonogram, and that phonogram is the one introduced at the beginning of the series in which the word occurs. Never tell the pupil a word in his phonic lesson, since only one new sound is introduced at a time, and the new step offers no difficulty if each foregoing page has been thoroughly learned. When it is necessary to indicate a certain sound in a word, call it by number—the second sound, the third sound, or whatever it may be.

Encourage pupils to whisper the sounds to themselves when they are studying a phonic or a reading lesson.

Encourage pupils to whisper the sounds to themselves when they are studying a phonic or a reading lesson. Without actually hearing the sounds they cannot get the blend and therefore cannot discover the word. It takes several months for pupils to be able to blend the sounds mentally. This whispering is not disorder. It is a necessary part of word-getting, and if checked too soon, the pupils' progress in word-getting may be greatly retarded. When the proper time for overcoming it has arrived, toward the latter part of the first year, pupils will naturally dispense with it because they will be able to get the word so quickly

The method presented in this book gives the pupil immediate mastery of a word taught and the words of its family, regardless of where he may find them.

through the eye that they will not wait for the assistance of the ear. An occasional request from the teacher that the pupil shall study to himself without moving the lips will overcome it without difficulty.

You may want to reserve a small space on the blackboard or use a flip chart for a permanent phonic chart. As pupils learn the sounds of the consonants, write them at the left in this space; and as each new compound phonogram is learned, write it at the right. This affords good material for reviews and word-building lessons conducted in the following way: The teacher points to a consonant, then to a compound phonogram, and pupils tell what word these would make if written together; or a pupil takes the pointer and indicates combinations that will make familiar words while either he or other pupils pronounce them.

The method presented in this book gives the pupil immediate mastery of a word taught and the words of its family, regardless of where he may find them.

Pupils should be taxed with the fewest possible rules. In this course only those are used which are simplest and most necessary for word recognition. Do not require pupils to memorize them; frequent application of the principles involved will ensure a thorough knowledge of them.

The separation of the family name from the initial sound greatly assists the pupil in acquiring the "blend." It becomes less necessary and is therefore used less frequently as the work proceeds. Strive for the "blend" at all times. The pupil's power to discover new words depends upon his ability to blend the sounds of which they are composed.

Constantly require pupils to apply their knowledge of phonics to their reading lesson; that is, do not tell the pupil a word in his reading lesson that he is able to get for himself. The habit of "making the sounds tell the word" must be thoroughly fixed. Thus the pupil will daily become more reliant, and after a few months his general knowledge of phonics will enable him to recognize many words containing sounds beyond his phonic training.

When a word occurs in the reading lesson that does not conform to the rule, such as *have*, *give*, etc., and the pupil pronounces it incorrectly, ask him if he knows such a word; when he replies that he does not, tell him there is something wrong with his vowel. He will immediately correct it and will soon learn to expect "exceptions," and to try another sound of a letter if his first sounding does not give him a familiar word, or a word that "makes sense" in the context.

If a word, unusually long yet containing only sounds previously taught, occurs in the reading lesson and seems difficult for the pupil, assist him by writing it on the blackboard and underscoring each compound phonogram or family name. Also teach him to put a finger over such a word, moving it off slowly so that he sees only one family name or one syllable at a time. This may be well demonstrated to the class by using a long narrow strip of pasteboard with which to cover the word on the blackboard and removing it in the way described above. When the teacher discovers a weakness in a phonic principle previously taught, she should promptly refer the pupil or the class to a lesson that demonstrates that principle. If it is a forgotten phonogram, the pupil should be given a quick review of the family of words in which that phonogram is the common element.

Make up sets of script phonic cards for seat work. Write four or five families in as many columns on each card. Write the initial consonant sound in red ink and the compound phonogram or family name in black. Then write the consonant sounds again in red on strips of pasteboard, and on other strips write the family names in black. Cut these strips up so that there is one consonant or one family name on each card. Pupils use these small cards for building families of words to correspond with those on the large card. Keep the small cards and the corresponding large one in the same envelope. When desired, the pupils may use the large cards for study or for copying. Each large card should be numbered on the back to correspond with the number of the envelope in which it belongs. Write on the outside of the envelope the name of each family included in the envelope; then it will not be necessary to look into the envelope in order to know what work the envelope contains.

When the teacher discovers a weakness in a phonic principle previously taught, she should promptly refer the pupil or the class to a lesson that demonstrates that principle.

When pupils have had a few weeks' practice in writing, begin conducting phonic spelling lessons, in order to reinforce the power to recognize compound phonograms. Write a family name on the blackboard, such as **-as** or **-at**; write it several times, one under another, making a column; now pronounce this family of words—*cat*, *bat*, *fat*, *last*, *mat*, *rat*, *pat*, *sat*, requiring different pupils to go to the blackboard and prefix the sound which makes the word. Or write on the blackboard the compound phonogram which is to be the common element of the series, then have the pupils copy it on their paper. Now pronounce the words, having students write as the words are pronounced. The ability to recognize compound phonograms as wholes, without separating them into their elementary sounds, greatly shortens the process of word recognition. This also serves to impress phonic principles upon the minds of the pupils and teaches them to apply those principles to all spelling, thus making spelling a matter of reasoning.

Pupils should be taught to look over a spelling lesson when one has been assigned that is made up of words of different families and determine the "dangerous places" in the words. For instance, in a spelling lesson of ten words, seven of those words may be strictly phonetic; that is, they may be governed by phonic principles and be spelled as they sound. The pupil does not need to waste time on these. But in the remaining three he finds unphonetic elements, so he studies only those three "exceptions." It is a good plan, in teaching children how to do this, to write the spelling lesson on the blackboard, making in red chalk the letters on which pupils are likely to trip. Some teachers have aptly called these "red danger signals."

If the pupils are taking up this course in the fall after having had part of the work the previous year, they should take a rapid review of the pages up to the point where their new lessons begin. When pupils enter the class from schools in which this phonic course has not been taught, the most satisfactory method of preparing them for work with the class is to take them rapidly over the work which the class has covered.

Whether pupils complete this course in one year, one and a half years, or two years, when they have completed it, their ability to read anything they can comprehend is assured. Each pupil should keep the course in his desk for ready reference, general reviews, and drills, as required, until the close of his third school year.

Florence Akin, 1913

*The words in this book are grouped according to their pronunciation in *Webster's New International Dictionary*.

— Florence Akin, 1913

**Classical Phonics* has been revised using the *American Heritage College Dictionary*.